PSYCHIC

TO

PROPHET

A Journey of Transformation

MICHELLE SEIDLER

Elani
PUBLISHING
A PRINT, DIGITAL & TECHNOLOGY COMPANY

PSYCHIC TO PROPHET

Copyright © 2019 by Michelle Seidler.

For information contact :

http://www.elanipublishing.com

Book and Cover design by Kinsey Moore
Cover Photography by Through the Lattice
ISBN: 978-0-578-49505-7

First Edition:April 2019

CONTENTS

To the reader

I am humbled that you have chosen to read this book about my journey.

This is not my story in entirety, what you will read here are the points where true transformation happened in me.

My prayer for you as you read the words in this book is that you would see Jesus and how He is revealing himself to you on your journey. That you might find yourself through my story and discover the why He is doing something, behind the what He is doing in your life. I pray that as you read, you are filled with courage to go with Him wherever He is leading you. And, where there has been fear holding you back, it will fall off, and faith would arise.

I pray that love for the beautiful Man, Jesus will arise in you like never before, and that a hunger for more would be imparted. And above all, I pray that by the Holy Spirit through this book you would receive a Grace to trust Jesus like you never have. May you be filled with LIFE! LIFE in Jesus' name that brings you forward into more of who you truly are!

Come Holy Spirit and reveal Jesus.

Dedication

With much love I dedicate this book to my daughter and son-in- law, Kasey and Joel Dobbins. This book was first written for you and the generations after me that you will bring into this earth. This book would not have happened without your support. You are my greatest gift. My desire and daily prayer is that my ceiling will be your foundation.

Introduction

MY MOM TOOK ME IN ONE DAY, and we stumbled into a woman's office who worked there in the town. She was a clairvoyant, which is New Age term that's comparable to a seer. 'Clairvoyant' simply means clear seeing. And clairvoyants, basically, are ones who see. My mom made an appointment for me to meet with her.

She did a type of seeing where she would take something that you wore, or something that you had on you all the time like your keys, and she would put it in her hands. She was basically tuning into your energy, and through that was her connection point to see. I gave her something of mine. I think it may have been keys, and she started to tell me who I was. Claire was her name. Oddly enough, the thing that I remember Claire saying was,

.

STEPPING INTO THE NEW AGE WORLD

"You know, when you get older, you're going to do what I do." She said, "You're a seer." I can't explain to you what it did to me in that moment. It was like my whole life made sense. I realized that there were people like me.

It wasn't so much of what she said to me. It was profound. It did deeply impact me, but being in that place, it was affirming to me that I wasn't crazy and that there were other people like me. Meeting her did that for me. Seeing what she was doing and that she could see me and that she could see my future and she wasn't crazy, it was like, *Oh, my gosh. These are my people, and this is who I am.* When she said to me, "You're going to do what I'm doing," it was like my whole life in that moment made sense.

It changed my life. It brought another level of peace to me in my identity. It silenced the lie, to a degree, that I was crazy. I would have several more years of the fear of being deceived, but the feeling of being alone and that I was crazy ended that day. For several years after that, Claire became someone that I met with regularly. She discipled me in a sense. This was where my journey into the New Age started.

Since I was young, I had a deep longing and desire to help people. Not knowing who I was or what I was called into I found myself helping people with the gift God had given me to see but as a psychic. Little did I know that I would soon encounter The One who gives gifts to all men and that He would take me on a journey of knowing and falling in love with Him. This journey would not only awaken me to the reason He gifted me the way He did, but I would discover an even more beautiful reason of why I was created: to freely give my life to The One who loves so generously and gave His life for me.

Jesus, thank you for seeing me, rescuing me, consistently fighting for me, calling me, and believing in me. You love me so well. You truly are an apple tree in the midst of the forest. You are fairer than the sons of men. You stand apart from the rest. You were there when I was left alone. You are the steady one. The one who remains, and never leaves. You have always told me the truth. You own my heart. Now and forever.

Chapter 1

Gifted Child

*There were clues to being different, but who knew what it
meant to be a gifted child...*

I grew up in a military home. My dad was in the air force, and we
traveled around a lot. Every few years, we were in different places.
It was just me and my sister and my parents. I grew up in a family
that was very dysfunctional. There was a lot of anger, a lot of
yelling, a lot of screaming. For all children, this is detrimental, but
for prophetic seer children, it's even more so.

The earliest memory that I have, related to this topic, is
probably around five or six years old in a psychologist's office. I
distinctly remember her asking me questions about the different
things that I was seeing, asking me to draw pictures, asking me if I
knew names because I was seeing things. I remember at the time not
really understanding what was going on but just, really like a child,
innocently answering her questions. At this young age I would find
myself in different psychologists' offices as we moved every few
years. At that time, I would say, I didn't experience a lot of demonic

activity. It was more angelic activity. I knew they were angels, but they came more in the form of looking like men or women.

As I got a little older, I distinctly remember the time my experience of knowing things started to grow. I was still seeing different things, but I remember starting to really know things that you couldn't know in the natural. One of the greatest troubles that came along with this was that I never really had much of a filter when it came to communication with others.

When I knew something, I spoke it. This created a lot of issues in the family. I remember them trying to hide things from us, but I just knew when something was a lie and would confront it.

> *With the prophetic, what you see a lot of times, your filter, has a lot to do with what goes on in your inner life. When you have a lot of trauma or abuse or negative environments, it really does open you up more to seeing in the darker realm versus the light.*

My parents divorced and this ushered me into a lot of emotional instability. I didn't know at the time, but I was really absorbing everything around me. As a seer, you experience all your senses in a heightened way. It's like your body is a sponge. Again, of course at that time, I didn't know that. It really started to increase around the age of eight or nine as the trauma from my family life just sent me into another place emotionally where I was completely unstable because I was absorbing the trauma of everyone around me. I was angry one minute. I was sad the next minute. As I got to ten, eleven and twelve years old, I became severely depressed and attempted suicide several times.

During this time, I really started to see and experience more of the demonic realm of things, where in the middle of the night, I would wake up and see demons. At this point in my life, they never affected me physically. I would see them in my room watching me. They never said anything to me. It was always just that they were watching me. It would really scare me when I would wake up and see them; I would jump out of bed and turn the light on.

As children, we think that everyone is like us. I thought that everybody experienced what I experienced. I thought everybody knew things. I thought everybody saw things. I began to discover that really was not true.

It was at this point where I started to battle with what was real and what was not. The enemy always tried to tell me I was crazy. Of course, when you're seeing psychologists, you start to realize this is not normal. I battled between what's real and what's not real because of what I saw in the spirit realm. What I was experiencing in the spirit realm was very real to me.

Then you have society telling you there's something wrong with you. Yet, at the same time, the things I knew became reality and were confirmed through different circumstances. I was in this constant battle over reality and not knowing if what I was really seeing and feeling was real or if I was being tricked. For so many years I always had a fear of being tricked, lied to, and deceived.

Fear became a lot more apparent to me as I got older. I probably could not identify it or call it what it was at that time, but it was fear that led me into a lot of depression and feeling alone. It was fear coupled with the fact that I was absorbing my environment and feeling all the emotions of everyone around me.

When I was thirteen, my mom, my sister and I moved to Florida where we had family. That was when a lot of things started to change and when I started to enter the time of being in and out of mental institutions.

UNDERSTANDING THE SEER GIFT IN CHILDREN

To circle back to the understanding of the gifting of the seer, I want to interject some takeaways here. Seers are prophets with a gift of discernment. So, when you have children who are seers, they absorb everything like a sponge. Their senses are super heightened, so they become like a sponge that absorbs everything. This is not just through the spiritual eyes of being able to see things but the hearing, the feeling, the smelling, the tasting. All of their senses are heightened. As seers we experience Him through all the senses. The challenge really is living and being aware of two realms at the same time. The dominant sense is different for everyone, but typically the seeing realm is the dominant sense.

I have a lot of people, to this day, who reach out to me with children who are sometimes prophetic, sometimes seers asking for help. The one thing that I tell them, and it is the most important thing to do with your children, is to teach them how to gaze on Jesus. Teach them how to get into that *place* and actually see Him. The way this works is you start with His nature. For example, you take an aspect of His nature, and you bring the children into focusing on seeing who He is using their imagination. So, let's say we select the aspect of His character that is mercy. We meditate on this aspect of His nature by looking at a story in Scripture that demonstrates this dimension of who He is.

For example, using the story of the woman caught in adultery in John 8, you can bring the children into seeing the mercy aspect of His nature. Then through gratitude and thanksgiving, they are actually looking at Him. They can begin to verbalize, "Jesus, thank You for Your mercy. You're so full of mercy to that woman who was caught in adultery. You didn't judge her. Your heart was just so in love with her that You moved in mercy." Guide them in those kinds of examples where all their focus is on the person of Jesus.

It's so essential for seer children to be rooted in that because they become like sponges, and they absorb everything around them. Their eyes are opened to the truth that, for example, if they're in a place of dysfunction in the family, they become a lot more susceptible to demonic spirits. That's what they're going to absorb, and that's what's going to affect them. That's what they are going to see because that's their environment.

Even parents of children who grow up in Christian homes (and countless people have reached out to me about this) say things such as, "My children are having nightmares. My child is seeing demons." And I'll say, "Listen, just do this. Get them to see Jesus." It roots them, and it keeps them from being really open more to the enemy. Essentially that's what happened to me because I grew up in a place of dysfunction. It made me so much more vulnerable and open to seeing more of the demonic realm and being affected more by that realm.

As I got a little bit older and into my pre-teen years, I was so open to that realm because of that dysfunction that it made me open to suicide. For me, at that time, that was the primary thing that affected me. I think for any child, they're going to be affected that way. It's going to affect them emotionally. A child just doesn't grow up in that environment and not be negatively affected. It just multiplies when you have a seer child because it affects them that much more in the spirit realm because, essentially, they're more open to the spirit realm.

As a child, you don't realize that's what it is. You think you're normal. When you're a seer you need to learn how to be dialed into the right channel, so to speak. Of course, as a child, you don't know that. You have to be trained in that. You have to be directed in that because you are dialed in automatically, in a sense, to your environment and the spiritual atmosphere of your environment.

I tell parents it's essential for seer children to learn how to dial into the correct spirit, the Holy Spirit, to the Person of Jesus. Teach them to look at Him.

For me, as a child, I was just dialed into the anger, the depression, the different negative things in my environment. That was my dial even as I got a little bit older. As I aged some, I started to be more affected by the demonic realm. I wasn't seeing angels or anything that was good. It was all dark. And why? It was because that was where my dial was tuned. And, so again, I tell parents it's essential for seer children to learn how to dial into the correct spirit, to the Holy Spirit, to this person of Jesus. Teach them to look at Him. Guide them in His nature to see His face because you want them tuned to that right channel.

GROWING UP GIFTED & CONFUSED

As I entered my preteen years, I ended up falling in with the wrong crowd, doing drugs and getting into a lot of trouble. At that age, my experiences of absorbing everything around me were intensifying. I was around so many people that were angry. The friends, the group that I was in, all around me were just angry. In my home life, my mom was in school full-time; she was getting her master's degree in psychology. She was working for the sheriff's department as a rape activist, so she worked with rape victims. She would get called out any time there was a rape, so she was rarely around. She was really trying to rebuild her life, but I was running wild.

I got increasingly more and more depressed and more and more angry. At that time, I started to experience more things at night with demonic activity. It was always traumatizing for me at night, seeing these things and not knowing what to do with it. Being a very verbal child, I didn't withhold anything; I had no filter. If I saw something, it would come out. At that age, at school, it got me in a lot of trouble. When I started getting into trouble with the police, or even with people around me, I knew exactly what was going on with them.

My experience was being very verbal and not holding anything back. I would tell my mom that I was seeing these demons at night.

At that same time, along those same lines, I knew things about friends and people around me, and I would tell them. It was never necessarily encouraging or good news; it was more about their issues. It was like, "You have this; you have that." "This is going on at home." "That's going on at home." It really created conflict in my life, even with the police. My mom, who was struggling to restart life for us and was trying so hard as a full-time student and working mom, had no idea what to do with me.

This is when I started once again seeing psychologists and psychiatrists. There were countless counselors, psychiatrists and psychologists. My mom had me see this one psychiatrist who worked with youth. He did these groups once a week where all the kids came together, and we'd talk about stuff in the group. I would sit in that group, and I would tell everyone in the group what their issues were. Any time my mom's insurance would run out, the psychiatrist would say to my mom, "Just keep bringing Michelle because she really gets the group going." I was in there helping the psychiatrist by getting the group started up saying, "Here's your issue.." It made them all very mad at me.

Again, that's just another example of how I would experience a lot of misunderstanding and a lot of rejection and just not have any clue how to process what was going on inside of me. I was thinking that we were just a bunch of kids in a group, and the goal was to talk about our stuff and the different things going on with us. I would just tell people, "Here's the issue. You with your mom or you with your dad, this is what's going on. Here's the issue. This is what you're doing; this is what they're doing." It really worked against me in a lot of negative ways.

I remember the psychiatrist saying (and many of them saying to me after that) that I had a lot of insight into my problems and everyone else's problems. I worked with him in that, but the issues at that time of just calling things out, knowing things, having demons visit me, and my mom being so busy and not knowing what to do with me created a lot of conflict. I also did not want to be controlled. I was rebellious, and I think a lot of that came from feeling abandoned. From the age of five to twelve, my parents were divorced twice. I lived with my Mom, then I lived with my dad, and then he sent me to live with relatives. Afterwards, I began living with my mom again. Through this, I formed real abandonment issues.

Chapter 2

The Lost Years

I was in and out of mental institutions, but the seed of the Gospel was planted.

I will never forget the first time I was put in the Florida Hospital psychiatric unit for youth. That night in a room with two beds, I was the only one there and felt the utter loneliness and abandonment of being left somewhere. It was so quiet, and I'll never forget laying in that bed and counting the tiles on the walls and feeling so empty, numb, and abandoned. That was when they really started medicating me a whole lot more.

Everything was very structured. You got up at six in the morning. You had breakfast, and they had different school type activities like horticulture and art. Every day was full of those kinds of things and then meeting with a group of doctors. I can look back and see how this was a subtle way that New Age thinking was introduced to me by one of the nurses in the hospital. Her heart really was to help.

She was very kind and really cared, and she gave me a little Walkman, a tape playing device with earphones. At night I listened to meditations that she gave me. She also had us doing meditations as a group. We would lay down in this big room, all of us, and they'd turn the lights off. She would lead us into the meditations. She brought me books on Shirley MacLaine at the time about aliens and reincarnation, and I became really fascinated with it. It started to shape my thinking in a new way. It shows the profound impact that nurses or teachers can have on children. It started to prepare me for a new direction.

I would go in and out of this one hospital several times, for months at a time. I was in and out of that place probably nine or ten times in a few years. It's quite funny now, but at that time, over the years, I held the record for being the one that was there the most. All the doctors and nurses knew me. My frequency there was a running joke. Although at Florida Hospital my experiences were of abandonment, I made friends. Even though it was a traumatic experience, it was as pleasant as it could be in that place.

I would get to a point sometimes where my mom's insurance would run out for the year, and the doctor would want to put me somewhere. When that happened, I went into the state hospital, which was where they put anyone with severe mental illness. It was not just youth; it was all ages. I would say that was where a lot of the trauma originated. Because of the lie the enemy was trying to drill into me at that time, I remember wondering whether or not I was crazy. The question of 'what was real/what was not real' was plaguing me. Because I was seeing things in the spirit realm, my mom would practice her psychology stuff on my sister and me for school. I think that was what fueled a lot of her wanting to have me locked up; she thought she knew the criteria.

When I would go into the hospitals, the doctors would ask me, "Do you see things?"
"Yes."

"Do you hear voices?"

"Yes."

"Are the voices telling you to hurt yourself or hurt other people?"

"No."

I remember being stunned by that question. They asked patients all those questions, and I fit the criteria as one who needed to be locked up. I never heard voices telling me to hurt myself or hurt other people, but I was in deep depression at the time, too. This is when I started to feel darkness around me all the time. I felt oppression. I attempted suicide many, many times. That got worse the more that I got locked up. Then I would go home and go back into school.

I was doing drugs when I was home, but I never got like a lot of my friends who became addicted. It just wasn't me. It wasn't really my thing. Looking back, I was kept from a lot of that stuff, but school didn't work for me. Even at school, I would skip class and head to the smoking section where we would get high.

I skipped school all the time. I simply didn't go to school. When I wasn't locked up and was supposed to be in school, I was skipping school. The school experience just didn't really exist for me. During middle school and high school, I was in and out of different institutions.

The first time that I was put in the state hospital was very traumatic because I walked in and thought, *this is no youth group here. This isn't a bunch of troubled kids. This is another realm of crazy.* I was so sad. I couldn't understand why I was there. I could not decipher what was wrong with me to the degree that I was in that place. The enemy would say, *you're crazy.* As professionals asked me questions regarding seeing things or hearing voices, I answered,

19

"No." I learned that equals crazy. Internally, I was in the battle over 'crazy' because the truth was: I was seeing things; I was hearing things; I knew things. I started to be quieter about it because I knew it got me in trouble.

In those places, they didn't hesitate to stick you with a needle and put you in a padded room by yourself. The first time I was put in the state hospital, I was there maybe two days when my mom came to visit me. We sat at this little table in the commons area just for two people, and I was sitting across from my mom. I was quiet, but I was crying. Tears were coming down my face. With a quiet voice I asked, "Mom, why am I here?" One of the nurses saw me crying and called the other nurses, and they came and got me and took me away from my mom. I'll never forget the moment of them grabbing me out of the chair as my mom was sitting there. I was so stunned and shocked. I felt a deep, deep sense of injustice. I had no understanding as to what had happened. That was the question of everything in my childhood.

As they were literally dragging me away from my mom, I was looking at her and screaming, feeling that abandonment and that deep betrayal. I so wanted to understand when I was sitting there with her. I just wanted to understand, and that's why I was crying. *Why am I here?* They removed me simply because they saw tears. I felt this sense of injustice, betrayal, and lack of understanding. They took me, and they tied me down on a bed in a room where there was nothing but a camera on me. My arms were tied down, my legs were tied down, and I don't think I have ever felt the feeling of injustice like I did that day.

I was screaming and yelling, "What are you doing? Why are

you doing this?" I couldn't understand. All I was doing was crying. They kept me there for three days with that camera on me, and I'll never forget I just yelled at that camera. It was so traumatizing, that sense of feeling like I had no voice. The depth of misunderstanding and not understanding was so intense. The word that I would put over it is 'injustice.' I knew it at that time. That was why I was screaming; I knew it was wrong. I knew it was okay to cry. Some people in that situation would have the message that it would not have been okay to cry. *You don't cry. You just be quiet. You don't cry.*

That never happened to me. Something that really worked against me through my childhood was I had a sense of knowing things. I knew when things were wrong when it came to people. I was never compliant. I didn't nor wouldn't comply to injustice. I fought it. I was always a fighter. I always bucked up to those things, and even when it got me in more and more trouble, I wasn't silent about it. Internally, it brought me into a lot of depression.

After three days they released me. Anyone who's been through abuse has this sense afterwards of an emptiness, like a brokenness. You're broken. Something's been stripped from you, and you're just empty, like a numbness. That was what I felt. I was so melancholy; I was very quiet. I kept to myself. In that place, people were literally not in their right minds. I remember thinking to myself, *Is this me? This must be me.* I knew these people weren't right in their minds, and if I was there, it must have been true about me as well. Again, it was a seedbed for so many lies.

I never stayed in the state hospital for more than thirty days at a time because that was the max amount of time that anyone could stay. That is the place I would go any time I had a year where my mom's insurance ran out. Basically, my mom's insurance paid for Florida Hospital adolescent unit, but when her insurance ran out, they put me in a state hospital, where you don't need insurance. That was kind of a threat a lot of times used over me... *you're going to go back to the state hospital.* But honestly, I was one of those children who did not think very much, and I didn't care. I just really didn't care about any of that. In and out of the adolescent unit, I would go home. Then I'd get in trouble with the police. I was running around with the wrong group, and I was in juvenile detention centers at the same time for being mouthy with the police. It was minor trouble; nevertheless, it was a toxic environment. Even though I would get in trouble with that group, I kept myself from doing some of the things that they would do. But the police and the hospitals knew me. I would go from the adolescent unit to home, get into some kind of trouble, go back into the adolescent unit and all while seeing counselors, psychologists, and psychiatrists.

There are so many stories I could tell about the state hospital, but here's a funny one. With me having a mouth, I held nothing back. I was sitting in the common area in the state hospital where everybody played cards; that's what they did. It wasn't like the adolescent unit where you had structured activities and school, horticulture, art or anything like that. The state hospital was where you just hung out in the common area, and primarily people played cards. I remember this one day, I was playing cards, and I saw this guy come into the common area. He had my underwear on his head, like a hat. I screamed, "You have my underwear on your head." And he said, "No, this is my hat." And he meant it. I said, "No, that's my underwear on your head." He had gone into my room and dug

22

through my drawers and got my underwear and put it on his head. The nurses came and got him and put a needle of something in him while he was screaming, "This is my hat! You can't have my hat!" This was one of those times where someone got put in the room. It literally is a padded room, and there's a little window on the door. You could hear people when they were in there. This guy, all night long you could hear him howling. He was just howling, literally like a wolf, all night long and talking about his hat. That was more of a funny experience.

I had another experience that was really more bizarre, spiritually. My roommate was a lady. She was probably in her forties, and she was in the common area. She had OCD that seemed really bad. She walked around with a towel, and she was wiping everything down all the time, super obsessive and cleaning, cleaning, cleaning everything. Everything needed to be clean. Though she was my roommate we did not talk, she didn't really talk to people, just obsessively cleaned things all the time. She would pace the floor, back and forth at night in our room. The first night I yelled at her until I fell asleep. The second night she did it, and I just screamed at her again. And all she would say, pacing back and forth, was, *thank you, dear Jesus, thank you, dear Jesus.* I screamed vulgar things at her, calling her names, *shut up, I need to sleep,* and for hours she continued. Well, I fell asleep eventually. The next morning, I woke up, and she wasn't there. She was gone, and I didn't really think anything of it. I thought maybe the doctors or nurses had her. Come to find out she had literally disappeared, and I was being interrogated by nurses, by doctors, by police as to where she had gone. They were looking at the vent; *could she have gone out the vent?* She literally disappeared. To this day, it is one of the most bizarre things I have experienced because all I remember her saying for hours was "thank you, dear Jesus."

I believe she was just wanting Jesus to take her out of that place, and I think He did. There's no way you can get out of that state hospital. You can't get through a door. They are heavy, like those heavy, cement, locked doors. You don't walk out of that place, and there are bars on windows. You don't get out of there. They were so perplexed. There was no way she got up through that vent. The vent wasn't messed up. That was quite a freaky experience for me, spiritually. It was not because I felt anything, but it was like, *wow, huh, she got taken.* But at the time for me, my whole world was reincarnation and Shirley MacLaine and aliens. I believed that people were being abducted by aliens and taken on spaceships because that was common back then. I thought (even though I know she was saying, *thank you, dear Jesus*) maybe the alien got her. That was my thinking.

Again, that was my experience from about thirteen to seventeen. That was the rhythm. The Florida Hospital, coming out, getting in trouble, doing drugs, skipping school, getting in trouble with police and then going into the state hospital was the cycle that I did for all those years. Honestly, there were some traumatizing experiences, but for the most part it became my normal. It becomes your culture; it becomes your life. It becomes-- this is just what happens.

I think because I was so medicated during that time, I really wasn't seeing a lot at all, like the demons, all of that. I still knew things about people. As a seer it's not just about the seeing, it's about all your senses, your feeling. You can smell ... I can smell spirits. I can taste them; they have a taste. I can feel it in my body. My body reacts to certain spirits, and that was certainly very much happening. But the actual seeing things tapered down a little bit at that time. It seemed like when that tapered down, the feeling in my body really increased that much more. Like I said, when I was around angry people, I just got angry. When I was around sad people, I got sad. Literally my body was like a sponge soaking it all in.

So, at the age of sixteen, almost seventeen, I was placed in an unlocked group home, which was intended to be a long-term situation for me where I lived with other youth. This group home was more about doing life, regular life, and going to school together, doing outings together and that kind of thing. At this point in my journey, I was very angry, felt very misunderstood, and I just wanted to escape. I don't know that I consciously had those thoughts, but I was just running. I wanted to run. Run where? I don't know. There was anger, a lot of anger, and feeling rejected, abandoned and misunderstood.

After being there maybe six weeks, I had found more peace. But I just ran. It was the middle of the night, and there was nothing holding me back, nothing keeping me there. Like I said, it was an unlocked facility, and I had an opportunity to just run. I think after being in so many locked facilities and feeling caged and trapped, with an opportunity to run, I just ran.

I honestly did not know where I was going, as strange as that sounds. Looking back, a lot of times I didn't think through anything; I just did it. I found myself a few miles away and my ankle started to swell badly. I couldn't walk anymore. I sat down on a bench on a well-lit road. As I was sitting there, I looked up, and I saw a billboard that said 'Run away? Need help? Call this 1-800 number.' Not knowing what I was thinking but knowing that I couldn't walk anymore and that there was no one I could call, I called the 800 number on a payphone not far from the bench. I told them the situation: I was at a bench and my ankle had swollen, and I had nowhere to go. About twenty minutes later, a white van came and picked me up and took me to a house in Orlando.

When I tell people this part in the story, their jaws drop. I didn't think about consequences. I was fearless, reckless, and I just did things. I never stopped to think about who it was in the white van and where they were taking me. I would come to find out later that this was House of Hope. The founder is Sara Trollinger. As of today, they have Houses of Hope all over the country. But this was where she started, and this was her first house. It's similar to Teen Challenge, which focuses a lot on drugs, but House of Hope wasn't just focused on drugs. At that time, it was just for troubled girls. This was a three-bedroom house where I was taken in to one of the rooms. Two of the rooms were bedrooms that had bunk beds for girls that were staying there, and one of the rooms was Sara, the founder's, office. I was taken into her office, and I remember sitting across from her at this big desk. I'll never forget looking over to my left and seeing a picture of her and Ronald Reagan. In my mind, it legitimized her. She was a kind-hearted person that carried a lot of authority. I just remember feeling a lot of kindness and feeling authority on her life.

As I sat across from her, she asked me about what was going on and why I was on the run. I told her about the mental institutions and the home and the group home and how I just felt misunderstood and I didn't know where I was going. She proceeded to tell me about Jesus, and unfortunately, I don't remember what she said to me. But she presented the Gospel to me; she presented God to me. It was

26

really powerful for me. I don't remember her words, I just remember the presence of God. She asked me to pray with her. I prayed with her, gave my life to Jesus, and I was literally on the ground weeping because of this presence that I was feeling.

She couldn't keep me there at their home because she was at capacity of how many she was allowed to have in the house, so she called my mom. My mom came, and she sat down with my mom and told my mom that I wasn't crazy. She actually told my mom that I was gifted. She also told her that she didn't believe the institutions and group homes were helpful for me. Looking back, they really weren't. They did absolutely nothing for me. My mom heard her and really heeded her words. From there, my mom took me home. I wouldn't see Sara again for several years after that. When I did see her again, she asked me how I got that 800 number. I told her that I saw the billboard. She told me that they have never had a billboard! We laughed and were both greatly encouraged by what God did.

Leaving the House of Hope that night my mom still didn't know what to do with me. I honestly don't know that my mom knew that Sara prayed for me and led me to the Lord. It was obvious that she really believed what Sara was saying, but again, I don't think she knew what to do with me, and I think that was always my mom's challenge. My dad wasn't around, and it was just my mom and my sister. She was always trying to do the best thing. That was who she was. She was always helping people, but she didn't know how to help her own daughter even though she loved me. Besides working as a rape activist, she also began working with children who were dying of AIDS and their family members. I remember my mom on the phone, all hours of the day and night, just loving people and serving people, helping people, and counseling people through trauma. She was always trying to love people well. Even with my mom's best attempts to help me, I was about to take a very dark path.

Chapter 3

Life as a Psychic

Groomed to be a psychic. A pulling back of the veil of what it looks like in the New Age world.

So, walking away that night from the House of Hope, I went home with my mom. Two things happened to me that night. Firstly, the gifting in me, my ability to see and hear and to know things, went to a whole new level. Secondly, I had a degree of peace that I hadn't had before, although I wouldn't say it changed too many things in my life.

I was seventeen years old at this point, and my mom, wanting to help, took me to a witch town in Central Florida. It was maybe a thirty-minute drive from us, called Cassadaga. It was known as a witch town, and basically, there was every degree of New Age imaginable. There were mediums that did channeling. That is, they talk to dead people. And you could go and see mediums who call on the dead, and they tell you what the dead are saying. There are real dark witches that outright serve Satan, and I always say this: what I came to learn in that realm is that there are probably five percent of witches that actually know they're serving Satan. That five percent know they're giving themselves to darkness. Ninety-five percent of witches don't know they're serving darkness. That's how thick the deception is.

But there in Cassadaga, you had every realm. There was every degree of witch that you can think of, and then there were those that worked as healers. You could go and get different healing techniques that they would use, everything from reiki, different types of massages that did healing, and different types of psychics, tarot card readers. I mean, you name it. It was a place for every type of New Age practice, all in this town. People lived there. They worked there. There were restaurants. There were bookstores.

My mom took me in one day, and we stumbled into a woman's office who worked there in the town. She was a clairvoyant, which would be the New Age term that's comparable to a seer. 'Clairvoyant' simply means clear seeing. Clairvoyants, basically, are ones who see. My mom made an appointment for me to meet with her.

She did a type of seeing where she would take something that you wore, or something that you had on you all the time, like your keys, and she would put it in her hands. The idea of that was basically tuning into your energy, and through doing that it was her connection point to see. I gave her something of mine. I think it may have been keys, and she started to tell me what she saw about who I was. Claire was her name. Oddly enough, the thing that I remember Claire saying was,

.

STEPPING INTO THE NEW AGE WORLD

"You know, when you get older, you're going to do what I do." She said, "You're a seer." I can't explain to you what it did to me in that moment. It was like my whole life made sense. I realized that there were people like me.

It was profound. It deeply impacted me. Being in that place was affirming to me that I wasn't crazy and that there were other people like me. Meeting her did that for me. Seeing what she was doing and that she could see me and that she could see my future and she wasn't crazy, it was like, *Oh, my gosh. These are my people, and this is who I am.* When she said to me, "You're going to do what I'm doing," it was like my whole life in that moment made sense.

It changed my life. It brought another level of peace to me in my identity. It silenced the lie, to a degree, that I was crazy. I would have several more years of the fear of being deceived, but the feeling of being alone and that I was crazy greatly subsided that day. For several years after that, Claire became someone that I met with regularly. She discipled me in a sense. This was where my journey into the New Age started.

I began to study. I studied astrology, but not the basic things of astrology. It wasn't just the zodiac that I studied but a more focused form of astrology that bordered on the scientific aspects. It was understanding the planets. Even to this day, I believe that everything God has written, it says that He's written it in the stars. It's all written. Everything in creation is prophesying. I believe that where the planets were, where the stars were, when we were born and where we were born prophesies something.

I believe that the New Age world has taken that and twisted it. When you think of Daniel, for example, the magi, they were those that studied astronomy. In Israel today they still do it. I believe it is

Jewish mysticism, but that there's truth in it and that it prophesies. The New Age realm turned it into divination. I also studied numerology, and I believe it's the same with numerology. Numerology is the study of numbers and the meaning of numbers and how different numbers in our lives have different meanings.

I believe that if you study and understand the Hebrew language, you see that every letter has a number that tells a story. Again, I think numerology is something that God, in His design, created to prophesy something, but that was also turned into divination. I studied the tarot cards. What was interesting for me with the tarot cards was that I would start to use the cards, having studied and learned them well, and I would go off into visions.

There's a place where people see through the cards. The cards tell a story, and there's divination where you're laying down the cards while they are telling a story about someone's life or about a situation. If you're a seer or you have other types of gifting, you see through the cards; you see through the story. The cards are like a door.

But for me, I didn't need the cards. If I started to talk to somebody, I'd go into visions. By eighteen years old I had already learned a lot; I was very hungry for it. I felt this was my path, my journey, who I was, and so I completely gave myself to it. In the few years it got deeper and deeper. I went into deeper and deeper things. I was really good at what I did. After about a year and a half, I started to work as a clairvoyant, a psychic, but I was known as a clairvoyant.

A psychic is like someone that you go to that can tell your future, but there are different types of psychics, meaning there are different giftings and different ways that people tell the future. I was working as a clairvoyant just like Claire. I was a seer.

That realm is like a dark hole. It just pulls you in, and it's never enough. You're never satisfied. It's similar to the Kingdom and your relationship with Jesus where your hunger only increases. You're never satisfied. There's always more, but in Jesus you have a sense of peace. But there, hunger remains. In that realm it's the same, but it's dark. It's never satisfied, and there's never any peace. Still, I was always very hungry to understand mysteries and always searching and always looking. I didn't know what I was looking for, but I was definitely looking and hungry while never finding it in that realm. Though I had found a sense of peace regarding who I was, darkness was still with me. I was in and out of abusive relationships and then found myself pregnant at eighteen. Abortion was never even a thought. I was going to be a mother, and I knew I had to start to get my life more together.

One day, I happened to see an article in a newspaper that was looking for psychics. Back then the psychic hotlines were really popular. I called the number. Basically, you call the number, and you have to do what's called a 'reading' for the person that you are talking to so that they can judge whether you are accurate. If you are, you get a job, and I did. I did the reading, and I got the job. You would connect your phone number with their line, and when someone would call in on the psychic hotline it would ring your phone. That was my job. That was my day-to-day. I was working on that phone. It really fine-tuned my gift because I was using it more, and I got to a place fairly quickly where I was actually seeing dead people. When I was talking to people on the phone, I would see their dead relatives, and I would hear from them. During this time, I also started to get more involved in Orlando in the New Age community. I had business cards made, and I started to work at different events. I'd rent out a table with my little sign, "Psychic Readings," and people would come and get readings. I eventually started to teach at different events and speak at different events on how to see, as well as other things. I started to build a clientele locally where people would actually come to see me. People would make appointments with me, and I would give them readings. That was my life. It worked for me, being a single mom, because I was able to be home with my daughter.

I had relationships with several different bookstores where I would go in and teach classes and quickly became somewhat well-known as being very accurate. I never tried to make this happen, but the primary people that started coming to me were leaders. That was more of what I was known for, which is interesting. It's such a picture that the gifts and callings of God are irrevocable. Depending on how you're living your life and what king you're serving determines how those gifts and callings play out.

It's so interesting, my life now. I was performing my gift and calling in the enemy's camp, but it wasn't for the Lord. I look at my life now, and it's such redemption because I am walking in my true gift and my true calling. I work with leaders and teach people how to see, but how to see Jesus! At the time, I was being me; the unredeemed me was working in a gift and calling. In everything I did back then, I was functioning in my gift and calling but not in the Lord.

I remember the first time that I saw someone in the spirit who had passed away. A lady came to my house, and I was doing a reading for her. I had a vision of a man with a dog, but it wasn't just a vision. Visions in the Lord are very different than visions not in the Lord. They're visions, but they're different. I had this vision, but I knew it was real and that the person was real. It wasn't just a vision; a better way of putting it is that I was in a place. It's like Paul said, "Whether it was here or there I don't know, but I was somewhere in the spirit."

I was somewhere in the spirit, and I saw this man with a dog. It was interesting because I somehow knew he couldn't see me or know that I could see him. In the room where he was there was this really overwhelming sense of loneliness. I started to explain to the lady what I was seeing, and she started to cry and say that was her dad. The man never talked to me, but the fact that I saw Him brought a lot of hope and encouragement to her because I did have an understanding about him, even though he didn't talk to me. I was able to really bring encouragement to her. Those things started to happen to me quite often.

I had one experience where I was talking to someone, and I felt this presence that was overwhelmingly sad. It was so disturbing to me. It was not a calm sad, but an intense rush of hopelessness and sadness. This lady I saw in the spirit knew that I saw her, but her presence was so strong with this hopelessness and sadness that I knew that she had committed suicide. I said to the person in front of me, that I was speaking to, that I knew it was a woman, and I could explain a little bit of what she was like. I asked if she committed suicide, and the person said she did. In that place it was so overwhelming for me that I asked the lady in the spirit to leave. I actually blessed her and said, "Please leave," and she did.

Most of my encounters weren't happy even though sometimes dead people would say something that would bring hope or encouragement. It wouldn't just in general bring people hope and encouragement to know that they were hearing from their dead relative or that you even saw their dead relative or friend or whatever. It just brought a sense of encouragement to them.

I learned you can talk to and see those that had passed away like when Saul went to the medium to call up Samuel from the dead. Of course, the medium did call up Samuel, and Samuel said, "Why are you disturbing me?" We know God forbids that, to get counsel from the dead. A lot of people would say that it's demons that were pretending to be relatives. I don't believe it. I believe that those were real people that I was seeing and was really encountering real people who lived and were dead. Obviously, I was not doing these things by Holy Spirit. When our spiritual eyes are open, we can see. By Holy Spirit we can see those who have passed on, just as Jesus saw Elijah and Moses on the mount of transfiguration and was talking to them. Everything the enemy does is a counterfeit of the things of God.

These things were a big part of my experience, and it drove me into deeper realms of learning about magic. I started to practice and learn about magic. I remember at a very young age feeling the authority on my words. The sense of feeling that authority and knowing my words had power intrigued me so much, it was the main reason I wanted to learn about magic. It was not so much about power or control, it was about mystery. I would recognize that I would say things and they would happen, and I wanted to understand that more. I now know this is connected to the prophetic and the prophetic declaration, but back then it was a mystery to me that I wanted to know more about.

I went deeper and deeper into that realm, it was my world. Those were my friends. That was my community. That was my job. It was my life. It was my identity.

Yet, at the same time I had an overwhelming sense that I didn't belong. I just felt different from the people I was around. Some of the things they would do, I wouldn't do. I had a conscience. I'm not saying none of those people had a conscience, but there were places with witchcraft and magic and such that I saw some of my friends experience. Unconsciously, there was a boundary line for me in darkness, especially when it came to anything that was hurting people. My heart always was to only help people. I genuinely did what I did because I thought it was doing some good. I've always felt a compelling on the inside of me to serve people and to help them.

When anything came up that would hurt people, that was where it stopped for me. Although I had no issue trying to manipulate things through magic to get what I wanted. But, if I felt like it was hurting anyone, I stopped. There was one exception that completely scared me into never doing magic again. The boundaries that I had regarding these things made me somewhat feel like I didn't belong even though I had lots of New Age friends, and I was really involved in the community, I still had that sense of, *yes, these are my people, but they're not my people.*

ABUSIVE RELATIONSHIPS

All my relationships were destructive. I tended to find myself with men who really didn't understand me, they didn't understand the weird things that would happen to me. A lot of times, and even after I had my daughter, it seemed like the night encounters really became much more frequent. I just had a lot of weird experiences that men thought were weird, and I also attracted men who lied and who mistreated me. My relationships were always the perfect storm of destruction. For several years, I did have a relationship with someone who really loved my daughter. At that time, I was working in the New Age, trying to do school, raise my daughter, and maybe have a family. But the relationship was unstable. We were living together and then not living together. Even when we weren't together, he would still see my daughter. She knew him as Daddy; that was her daddy.

I'll never forget the last time I talked to him on the phone. I remember having such a weird sense and saying to my mom, "He acts like he's never going to talk to me again." He was talking about the strangest things and going on and on about memories of our relationship. He was being very nostalgic and wouldn't hang up with me, and I had started dating someone else at the time as well. I remember we were even talking about getting back together, but we were both in other relationships. It was a few days later that my mom told me she got a phone call that he was killed in a motorcycle accident. He loved motorcycles. He loved dirt bikes. He was definitely a risk taker and did all the wild stuff, but he was on his way to work, not driving crazy, on a rainy day when a truck hit him and killed him. He was 24 years old. That sent me into a dark, dark depression.

The new relationship that I was in was incredibly destructive. He lied to me all the time and was cheating on me. He would be cheating on me, and I would know by the spirit. I would see it, confront him, and he would tell me I was crazy. It was a lot of manipulation and lying, and I really began at that point to become so much more fearful about being deceived because I encountered so many lies in relationships. Then I would see and know the truth, but they would tell me I was crazy; that was the theme. People would lie; I would know the truth. I was told I was crazy for what I saw and what I knew to be true. I always eventually found out the truth about things. The truth always had a way of showing its face, and yet there was still this, "You're crazy." I mean that was the constant lie that was spoken to me but specifically through relationships. Honestly, since being a young child that was my constant dilemma.

This relationship became abusive as well, emotionally, mentally, and physically abusive. It was a destructive relationship, so when my previous boyfriend, my daughter's daddy, was killed, it sent me into a deep, deep, deep depression. I attempted to commit suicide, and I really thought that it was better for my daughter if I wasn't around. I was such a mess that I thought her life would be better without me. I just didn't know who I was. I didn't know what I was going to do, and I couldn't get it together. I had come to believe again that I was crazy.

I gathered some medication my mom was taking for some issues that she was having and took it. The next thing I remember is waking up in the hospital several days later. I have this memory of this time, not visual memory, but emotional memory of being with the Lord. I just knew I was, and I knew that He sent me back. They were surprised that I lived. I was unconscious for a few days, and they didn't think I would survive. When I was unconscious, I was with Jesus. I don't have visual memory of it, but I have emotional memory. After being in the hospital for a little over a week, they sent me home. The first thing I did when I got home was get on my knees. I said, "God, I don't know if you hear me, but I just want to help people."

During that emotionally and physically abusive relationship, he had beaten me up several times. He ended up in jail for kidnapping and attempted murder on my life. This would be the second boyfriend that had attempted to kill me. I didn't press charges against him, but the state did. Because I wouldn't press charges, he got out within a few months, and I was right back in the relationship again. It was just destruction. There were several years of me getting away and then getting back in it. We would live together and then not live together, continuously.

That was my life for several years with him lying to me, cheating on me, and I would know it. I could be in his presence, see someone around him, and I would confront him. He just always told me I was crazy, but I felt like I couldn't get away from him. When I would attempt to leave him, he would always find me and kind of lure me back. I feel like so much of it had to do with being under deception in my life. In that New Age world there's just a spirit of deception. It just covered every inch of my life, and I hated it.

I had this thing in me about truth, and seeing truth was like a speck of light in my life. In situations where I would get a glimpse of truth about something, it was like one percent, and the rest was ninety-nine percent deception. That one percent was just called crazy, and it was a prison for me. It brought a lot of depression, a lot of sadness. For several years, that was just my life, with my daughter growing up in that. I recognized the gift in my daughter at an early age as well. For her, it started with colors. She would see different colors on people. "Mommy, why does that person have this color on them?" I started to teach her things that I knew at a young age. She had her own little tarot cards at three and four years old. I wanted to teach her. I didn't want her to experience the things that I experienced, and she herself saw a lot of trauma in my relationship and experienced a lot of trauma when her daddy died. Then her mom attempting suicide was just a rough time for both of us.

INTRODUCTION TO KABBALAH

After several years of working full time as a clairvoyant and teaching classes in the Orlando area, I was speaking at a local New Age event, and I had a little booth as well. After I had spoken, I went back to my booth, and this man came up to me who was a very charismatic, African-American, light skinned male with beautiful green eyes, very striking. He said to me, "You're really gifted, and I have a group, a secret group that I would love for you to be a part of." And he gave me his information and told me about the group.

It was very intriguing to me. He used the word 'secret,' and it was a mystery, and I was always seeking. I was always searching, so this definitely got my attention. I went to his meeting of a group of eleven or twelve people, and they were studying Kabbalah. Kabbalah is Jewish mysticism and a major focus is learning what

God is. We would look at the tree of life and study what God is - the male and female attributes of God. Part of this learning is done using the Old Testament.

We used the Old Testament to study, but he also taught us magic, though they didn't call it magic. It was more about this place of learning to rule, which really is magic at the end of the day, twisting the truth of how we are called to have dominion and bring the Kingdom of God to earth. It's like miracles. We are called to partner with God to see miracles where we are changing the environment or a situation. That's the way we're called to do things by the Holy Spirit. But the opposite of that is magic and manipulating events to get something to happen. He was bringing us into how to move objects, manipulating matter, which is a big part of Kabbalah, and learning to rule over matter.

I went to a few meetings and it was intriguing to me. I was learning new things, and I'd always wondered about the Bible, although I hated Christians. I thought they were hypocrites. My mom took us to a church when my sister and I were younger and the pastor, who was married, tried to seduce my mom. She was devastated, and so were we. Any idea of Church was not appealing to me. I was intrigued by the Bible and what we were learning out of the Old Testament though. After going to a few of these meetings, when things were over and I would go home, I would get a little weirded out because at night when I would lay in bed I would feel this man's presence in the spirit watching me. I felt like he was trying to take something from me, steal the gift from me. That was the best way I can explain how I felt.

It started to bother me. You must understand in that realm,

you're just under such a deception that as a Christian you think…*this is good…this is evil…this is bad…this is good.* Well, the lines aren't so clearly drawn in that realm. I mean, that's the nature of deception. You would think I would know this guy was bad news, but I didn't. I didn't understand what I was feeling from this man like he was trying to take something from me. I was thinking to myself…*I wonder if he's bad,* because it just did not feel right.

During this time, I also had several other interesting things that were happening. I was having dreams that were different. I was having dreams of being in space. It was like something was happening to me while in dreams on the inside of me. I started to have an obsession with doves, and I was seeing doves in the spirit and talking about the Holy Spirit. Although I knew absolutely nothing about "the" Holy Spirit.

Now, in these meetings, we never talked about the Holy Spirit or Jesus or anything like that, so I didn't even know what I was talking about. I also had an experience where I walked out on my porch. I remember sitting there, and I saw myself outside myself. It was like me coming out of my body in the spirit. I came out; I could literally see myself standing in front of myself, and I said goodbye to myself. I'll never forget that day because it was so strange to me.

I thought to myself, *'Am I going to die?'* It was something beyond me; it wasn't my conscious mind. I saw myself come out of myself, stand in front of me and say goodbye. I had just different weird experiences that happened in a short period of time within a few weeks, all while feeling this guy visiting me at night and wondering whether he was bad. Well, one day I was pondering it and thinking about it, and I heard a voice. This voice was a different voice than I had heard before. And the voice said to me, "Ask him about Jesus." I just knew that this voice was telling me that if he said anything bad about Jesus, then he was bad.

That was my theology. You say anything bad about Jesus, you're bad. I shouldn't even say it was my theology; it was just this voice that was guiding me. During the next meeting I went to that week, we were in the Old Testament, and I said, "Well, here we are looking in the Bible. What about Jesus?" And he said to me, "Jesus never existed." And I said, "Well, what about the Bible? The New Testament?" He said, "These are just stories and examples in the way that we're supposed to live."

And I stood up, and I said, "You're a liar." I told everybody in that room that he was a liar and that they should leave. And I got my stuff, and I stormed out. Before I even got in my car, I immediately got sick and a high fever.

Chapter 4

Redemption

Oh! how He loves! When all hope is gone, He comes into the darkest places and redeems.

After my last Kabbalah meeting, I got home, and I was burning up with a high fever. I was super sick. If there was ever a time that I thought I was crazy, that was it. I was seeing angels; I was seeing demons. There was a war over my soul. I felt like I wasn't even there. It was like I was lost in it. I was experiencing the swirl of demonic and angelic activity, and this went on for days.

I had marks come on my body, on my hands. It was just a time of real warfare. I would go in and out of my closet, until finally, I came to the end of it. I was in my closet where I cried out to God. I said, "God, if you're real, come and help me." Shortly after that, again in my closet, things started to come out of my mouth that I could not comprehend. I grew up where my mom told us the devil wasn't real and hell wasn't real. It didn't exist.

I had no comprehension about hell or the devil or anything like that, but words started to come out of my mouth like, "I hate you, Satan." I literally said, "I hate you, Satan. I don't want to have anything to do with you!" And I just started renouncing different things out of my mouth. It was like bypassing my brain and just going through a renouncing of the devil. Holy Spirit was really taking me through deliverance.

This went on for a little while, and it was perplexing even to me because when it was happening, I was totally aware of the fact that it was coming out of my mouth. However, I wasn't thinking it. It wasn't coming from my understanding. Several hours went by, and then I went into a different experience. I saw in the spirit a literal dove come down from over the top of my head, and it entered me. Then I again started to say things out of my mouth that I couldn't comprehend.

I started talking about love, forgiveness, peace, and all these things were just flowing out of me. I started to write these things down. I was obviously aware that something was happening to me, though I did not have any idea what it was. When it all lifted, I felt completely different.

I remember stepping outside on my porch, and I felt lighter. The colors were brighter; I felt like a different person. I was new. I sat down at my table with that notebook I had written in, and I heard that Voice again, the Voice that I now know is Holy Spirit. The Voice that told me to ask the man about Jesus began to speak several things to me. He first said to turn myself in to the police. I had a warrant out for my arrest for different things. It was nothing terrible, but I just was super rebellious, and it was traffic stuff. So, there was a warrant out for my arrest, and the Holy Spirit told me to turn myself in. He gave me a list of people that I needed to forgive, some people to write letters to. Then He gave me a vision. In the vision I saw myself walking down the street, crossing the street, and walking into this store. I didn't know what was there, but I saw myself doing it. He said, "I want you to go there." So, I did. I started walking down the street where He showed me, and it was a used bookstore. He showed me where to go in the bookstore. I went to the back of the bookstore. On this top shelf all the way up, He told me to grab this book, so I did. I grabbed it, and it was a Bible. It was a used Bible.

There was another book that I grabbed that had a picture of a white dove on it. It was about the Holy Spirit. I went home, and I opened the Bible to the New Testament. I discovered the things that were coming out of my mouth were actually written in the Bible, and I heard Him say, "I'm the God of this Bible. Follow me." It was so impactful for me. Everything came together, and I knew in that moment that everything that I was doing was wrong in my life, particularly the New Age. I knew it because what I had encountered was the Spirit of Truth, and I fell in love. It was the reality of, *you shall know the truth, and truth shall make you free.* I had such an encounter with Truth that opened my eyes, and no one had to tell me that any of this New Age stuff was wrong.

I knew it was all wrong. I burned things. I threw things away. I cut off every single relationship that I had, and I fell in love with the Spirit of Truth. I had lived so under deception my whole life with not knowing what was true or what was not true. So, when truth came (and I knew it was truth) I fell so in love with the Spirit of Truth because it was true, pure, and it set me free. That truth for which I hungered for so long had come to me. He spoke to me and said, "You're a witness and a messenger of truth, and you're a witness and a messenger of light. And you will write books."

I had no idea what that meant, but I just started to follow that Voice. I started to get rid of everything in my house, every single book, and my tarot cards. I completely quit everything that I was doing cold turkey: the classes I was teaching, the working, the people that I was working with in the city, the readings that I was doing, my friendships. I also wrote a letter to the judge asking for mercy for the warrant out for my arrest. He granted it to me and reduced my sentence if I turned myself in right away. My daughter stayed with a friend while I went to jail for thirty days.

I took my Bible, and I just read my Bible in jail for those thirty days. It was like heaven. It's a weird thing to say, but I just devoured that Word and listened to the Holy Spirit and talked to the Holy Spirit. I had so many issues going on in my life. I remember thinking that what He wanted from me was to go to church and I said, "God, if You take care of all of this, I'll go to church for the rest of my life." And He did. He answered every single prayer. It was a season of miracles.

He did so many miracles and gave me such mercy and favor. It was the real start of a new life. While getting out of jail I made a commitment in my heart that I was going to serve Jesus and that I wasn't going back. And I never did.

KICKED OUT OF CHURCH

After my thirty days in jail, I was excited to start my new life. I really had my heart and my mind set on doing what I had said to the Lord that I would do; that was to find a church and go to church every week. So, I found a church. Come to find out, it was a fairly new church, less than a year old. It wasn't that big, but it was a charismatic, spirit-filled church. I had, I think because of my encounter with the Holy Spirit, the idea that church was just love and truth and all that's clean and good. It was a naïve perspective that I was going to go into church and that this was what the church looked like: the people were perfect and full of love, goodness, and kindness.

I was soon to discover that that was not true. I think my daughter and I were there a few months, and it was a powerful few months, when my daughter, who was six years old, decided she wanted to get baptized. We were in the car to one of the baptism services, and she said to me, "Mommy, I want to get baptized." I said, "No, I don't want you to get baptized because you really need to understand what you're doing. It's a really important thing, and I don't know if you understand what it means to get baptized. Let's talk about this."

She was disappointed and quiet, and the Lord spoke to me and said, "You let her get baptized. She knows what it means." I said to her, "Do you know what it means to get baptized?" I was stunned as she laid it out for me on what it meant to get baptized, that she was giving her heart and her life to Jesus. She wanted to do that, so she got baptized that day. It was a really good few months, and I had a deep desire to serve the church. That all came to an abrupt ending one day as we were sitting in the service, and the pastor's wife stood up in front of the church and said, "We have a wolf in sheep's clothing." She pointed at us and, basically, kicked us out of the church. I was devastated and asked her what we did. She said that she had found one of my business cards, one of my old business cards in Orlando somewhere, and knew my background. Because I had recently come out of that, she kicked us out of church.

Had the Lord not come to me in the way that He did I probably would've been so hurt that I would've left the church permanently, but I knew there was such a grace on my heart during that process because of the way the Holy Spirit had come to me. I knew He was good and kind. I knew that He had called me into His house. I knew that He loved me. I knew that what was happening was not Him. I knew they were just afraid and didn't understand. I didn't understand why they didn't come and talk to me and why they didn't want to talk to me. It was hurtful. It was hard, but I feel like it was just really such a grace on my heart that protected me. I don't feel like I got offended or bitter. I just said, "Okay, I need to find a different church," and I left. It was a big eye opener. Recently delivered psychics coming into a Church was not normal. I had seen a big sign for a church off the highway a few times and decided that I would try that church. It was a much bigger church, an Assemblies of God church, and we started going there. This church had a strong established deliverance ministry, and I immediately signed up for a very long process.

Chapter 5

Process

Oh! how it hurts! Process is long and not always easy, but we get to meet Jesus in profound ways as we learn His ways are not ours.

At that time, I really started to give myself to deliverance ministry since this was the focus of my church. I actually stopped having visions, and it was the first time in my life that I can remember not seeing things for that much of an extended time.

I would still sense things and know and discern things, but I wasn't having visions. The first deliverance program that I went into was twelve weeks long. It was basically where you would go to classes, read books, and at the end, you went on a retreat.

I got the books, and before I even went to the first class, I already started just having things happen. I'll never forget sitting in my room about to open the first book, and I literally could discern spirits leaving. I knew they were generational. I just knew by the Spirit. As spirits would manifest in my room and go, I knew that they were connected to my family.

It was a powerful time for me of deliverance and a lot of breaking of soul ties. A lot of it was related to traumas, childhood traumas, things that I had been through in mental institutions in my younger years, depression, suicidal tendencies, issues on my mom's

51

side, and issues on my dad's side. It was a few years of this. I was in a church where though they were really strong in deliverance ministry, they never talked about the prophetic.

In my mind, *I don't know why I came to this conclusion*, I thought that visions were bad. I threw out the baby with the bathwater. Basically, I concluded that everything I did in my previous life was bad, and that was just the bottom line for me. I didn't have a redemptive viewpoint at all. I didn't understand that it was a gift that God had given me: to see. I didn't realize that He had created this gift in me for His glory, for His purposes. I didn't know that yet.

I just despised what I was into so much that I wanted to have nothing to do with it. At that time, it was so evil to the point that even candles were evil to me. I mean, I went to the extreme. Any kind of incense, candles, or anything having to do with my previous life was bad, wicked, and evil, and I wanted nothing to do with it. I was zealous in that. That was my understanding, and so I just longed and yearned for righteousness and wanted to be clean.

As I was going through deliverance, I had a job that was paying me okay at the time. Really, I was just surviving, but that was my life. My life was my daughter, church, and deliverance ministry. That went on for several years. One day my daughter came to me and said, "Mom, I want to go to this other church."

She had made some friends through some activities in the city where churches came together. These friends were at another church, and she had really bonded with these kids and wanted to go to their youth meetings.

I thought to myself, "Well, if my daughter's hanging out with these kids, then I should really find out about this church and make sure that it's a good environment for her." I went to a Wednesday night service. As I walked into the church, the Holy Spirit spoke to me, "You are home." It stunned me because I loved the church where I was; I thought that was home.

I knew it was the Lord, but it was a difficult transition. I responded anyway. This new church definitely moved a lot more in the Spirit and little did I know that the Holy Spirit was taking me to school. I was about to enter school in a whole new way. After years of deliverance ministry, it was like the Lord said, "Okay, you're ready to move into a different realm." Clearly, I wasn't going to be able to move into that realm at the church I attended. This started a whole new journey for me.

I entered this new season of my life at a new church, and I was so zealous for righteousness. I was in love with God, with the Holy Spirit. I was the girl in the church who had always sat in the back, so free in worship. I was definitely a worshiper, even dancing. So many times, I would fall out under the Holy Spirit with no one laying hands on me. I was just so lost in worship and getting touched by the Lord, I would just fall to the ground under His presence. I was so hungry for Him and desperately hungry for more of what I was experiencing.

Several months after starting to go to this church, things started to happen rapidly with me in relation to my gift and seeing and hearing from the Lord. I always had a real passion for my city and the state of Florida, and it started for me in my room one day praying for the city. I had a vision about the city that startled me because I hadn't had a vision in a few years. It also devastated me. I had no understanding. The new church I was in moved in the Holy Spirit, and my pastor would prophesy, though I didn't make a correlation between speaking words of prophesy-what God is saying-with visions yet. I just didn't see any correlation. When I had that vision in my room about the city, my heart was broken. I wept and repented and said, "God, why isn't this gone from me yet?" I was just so devastated and ashamed. I had a broken heart, honestly, over that incident for a few days.

A few days after that, I was in a Christian bookstore, and I saw a book. It said, "Prophetic Intercession." The Holy Spirit drew me to it. It was like a manual, and I picked it up. I went home and read it, and it talked about visions. It was such a turning point for me of, *Wow! Okay. My visions are from God.* This is what you do with it. God was showing me visions and speaking to me about things so I can pray. That brought such freedom to my heart. It started me on a journey where I started getting words for the church, always encouraging words that I'd tell my pastor that they would release to the church. They were always good and encouraging words.

For the next year and a half, it was so much about going deep in the Holy Spirit. I did a lot of reading and studying, and honestly, partnering with the Holy Spirit. Even though the church I was in moved in the Holy Spirit and was open to prophecy, there was no training. At that time in the church, you really didn't hear a lot about prophetic training. Today, there's prophetic training everywhere. But at that time, you didn't hear a lot about it. Of course, back then we didn't have social media. If it wasn't in your city or you were not linked in with a certain ministry, it really wasn't accessible. For me, it really was just the Holy Spirit. He started to teach me. He would tell me, "I want you to sit here," when I would go to church. "I want you to sit here and watch this." He would speak to me in the Spirit about something, and I would watch it happen in the natural. Then He would talk to me about it.

This was a lot of what my life looked like at that time. He would put me in situations, show me things, and then confirm what He was speaking to me. It was really a time where He was building me up and encouraging me and encouraging my faith, building my faith with what I was seeing and what I was hearing. Even though I had gotten a lot of deliverance and a lot of freedom, I still had a bit of this fear of being deceived or lied to. Honestly, I would say ninety percent of it was gone, but the Lord was really using this time to encourage me that, "No, you hear from Me. I'm the One speaking to you in these visions."

It was training for me with the Holy Spirit building me up in my competence and my faith that it was Him that I was hearing from, and I wasn't crazy. It wasn't me; it was His voice. That season for me was a lot of those kinds of situations where it was Him really rooting me in the fact of that gift. In the New Age world there hadn't been a lack of confidence or questioning. When I was younger, it was, *am I crazy*, then I came into the New Age world. I was confident in what I was seeing and hearing because it was confirmed by people.

When I came to the Lord, I had those moments in that time where I thought the aspects of my gift were all evil. As I was starting out afresh with the Lord, it was like I needed a season of Him rooting me deeply in, *No, this is my voice. This is my voice. This is my voice. You hear my voice. This is me. This is me. This is me.* I can tell you countless instances where He was just being so intentional to put me in situations, and I was quiet usually. It was a time of watching, listening, and learning. Again, He was saying, "Go here," and would speak to me, and I would just watch. Then I would see what He would do in the natural, and I would say, "Yep, this is You. This is Your voice." It was a very intentional season of that for me for over a year; at least with countless situations where He established in me in a greater understanding that it was His voice that I was hearing. I was deep into prayer, and I served in prayer ministry in the church.

I spent hours alone with the Lord. It was like a time of rebuilding in a sense, in a small way. But I would say about a year and a half into this, I was really growing a lot by the Spirit. Then I started to encounter warfare at a level that I hadn't experienced before. Yet, I was aware that the Lord was allowing it. He had built me up enough on the inside to know that there were places that I could walk into at this point that I would be able to go through.

I hit a point where, suddenly, I just had ridiculous backlash and warfare. I would wake up in the middle of the night, and I would see snakes in my room. There were literal snakes in my room. I had TVs thrown at me in the middle of the night with no one in the room. A TV would just be lifted and thrown at me. I would wake up in the middle of the night in terror, with the demons again in my room watching me. I knew the enemy was very angry. I feel like I had broken into a new place in who I was in God and my identity, and I had just hit this place where the enemy knew I was about to break into an even newer place in who I was. All hell was breaking loose around me and in my home. I had lost my job. It just seemed like everything fell apart. As a result of all this, my daughter and I ended up homeless. We lost our apartment, and I just came to this point again where I had nothing.

I went to the church, and they helped us. A lady there at the church had a little older mobile home. God provided for my daughter and me, and we lived on this little campground in this trailer for a while. That went on for probably about six months. It was a time of my faith being encouraged where the enemy was really coming against me, but there was endurance being created in me to go through it. It was that James 1 count-it-all joy when you fall into various trials, knowing that the testing of your faith produces something. It produces endurance. It produces patience. Really, that's what that season was for me. In the natural it was loss. There was just warfare, trial after trial after trial, loss after loss.

I was moving in the Lord and trusting the Lord in that situation, keeping my worship through it all. I didn't take my eyes off the Lord. At the time, I didn't understand any of it. I didn't have any clue what was going on around me.

When you get free and you get deliverance, it's not like the devil rolls out the red carpet and says, "Okay, go on, see you later." However, I love how the Lord allows measures of these things in our life to strengthen us in Him. I had seen Him as the one who delivers me out from, but now I was seeing the one who delivers me "through."

I was in a Psalm 18 season.

I will love You, O Lord, my strength.

The Lord is my rock and my fortress and my deliverer;

My God, my strength, in whom I will trust;

My shield and the horn of my salvation, my stronghold.

I will call upon the Lord, who is worthy to be praised;

So shall I be saved from my enemies.

The pangs of death surrounded me, And the floods of

ungodliness made me afraid.

The sorrows of Sheol surrounded me;

The snares of death confronted me.

In my distress I called upon the Lord,

And cried out to my God;

He heard my voice from His temple,

And my cry came before Him, even to His ears.

Then the earth shook and trembled;

The foundations of the hills also quaked and were shaken,

Because He was angry.

Smoke went up from His nostrils,

And devouring fire from His mouth;

Coals were kindled by it.

He bowed the heavens also, and came down

With darkness under His feet.

 And He rode upon a cherub, and flew;

He flew upon the wings of the wind.

He made darkness His secret place;

His canopy around Him was dark waters

And thick clouds of the skies.

From the brightness before Him,

His thick clouds passed with hailstones and coals of fire.

The Lord thundered from heaven,

And the Most High uttered His voice,

Hailstones and coals of fire.

He sent out His arrows and scattered the foe,

Lightnings in abundance, and He vanquished them.

Then the channels of the sea were seen,

The foundations of the world were uncovered

At Your rebuke, O Lord,

At the blast of the breath of Your nostrils.

He sent from above, He took me;

He drew me out of many waters.

He delivered me from my strong enemy,

From those who hated me,

For they were too strong for me.

They confronted me in the day of my calamity,

But the Lord was my support.

He also brought me out into a broad place;

He delivered me because He delighted in me.

The Lord rewarded me according to my righteousness;

According to the cleanness of my hands

He has recompensed me.

For I have kept the ways of the Lord,

And have not wickedly departed from my God.

For all His judgments were before me,

And I did not put away His statutes from me.

I was also blameless before Him,

And I kept myself from my iniquity.

Therefore the Lord has recompensed me according to my righteousness,

According to the cleanness of my hands in His sight.

With the merciful You will show Yourself merciful;

With a blameless man You will show Yourself blameless;

With the pure You will show Yourself pure;

And with the devious You will show Yourself shrewd.

For You will save the humble people,

But will bring down haughty looks.

For You will light my lamp;

The Lord my God will enlighten my darkness.

For by You I can run against a troop,

By my God I can leap over a wall.

As for God, His way is perfect;

The word of the Lord is proven;

He is a shield to all who trust in Him.

For who is God, except the Lord?

And who is a rock, except our God?

It is God who arms me with strength,

And makes my way perfect.

He makes my feet like the feet of deer,

And sets me on my high places.

He teaches my hands to make war,

So that my arms can bend a bow of bronze.

You have also given me the shield of Your salvation;

Your right hand has held me up,

Your gentleness has made me great.

You enlarged my path under me,

So my feet did not slip.

I have pursued my enemies and overtaken them;

Neither did I turn back again till they were destroyed.

I have wounded them,

So that they could not rise;

They have fallen under my feet.

For You have armed me with strength for the battle;

You have subdued under me those who rose up against me.

You have also given me the necks of my enemies,

So that I destroyed those who hated me.

They cried out, but there was none to save;

Even to the Lord, but He did not answer them.

Then I beat them as fine as the dust before the wind;

I cast them out like dirt in the streets.

You have delivered me from the strivings of the people;

You have made me the head of the nations;

A people I have not known shall serve me.

As soon as they hear of me they obey me;

The foreigners submit to me.

The foreigners fade away,

And come frightened from their hideouts.

The Lord lives!

Blessed be my Rock!

Let the God of my salvation be exalted.

It is God who avenges me,

And subdues the peoples under me;

He delivers me from my enemies.

You also lift me up above those who rise against me;

You have delivered me from the violent man.

Therefore I will give thanks to You, O Lord, among the Gentiles,

And sing praises to Your name.

Great deliverance He gives to His king,

And shows mercy to His anointed,

To David and his descendants forevermore. (Psalm 18 NKJV)

After a few months I found a really good job in sales where I excelled and did well. My daughter and I were able to move into a nice apartment. I started to grow. I listened to a lot of Joyce Meyer at the time. It was a lot of my food. I got her tape of the month every month, which was a ministry that really spoke a lot into my life and helped shape me and know how to walk with God. I came to a good and stable place in my life.

But I had a constant inner turmoil about my life. I had this deep, disturbing aching that there was more for me in my life. It was this sense of calling, but I wouldn't have said it was a calling at the time. It was just really disturbing and made me discontented. It was something I cried over all the time. Even though I had a good job and things were going well externally, I knew that wasn't my life. I would cry daily on the way to work. *If life is nine to five, for me it's just not how I was made. And if my life is nine to five, God, just take me now.* It was death for me.

God, who am I? There was this constant wrestle over who I was. *What about the way you made me, with these gifts?* Throughout all these different seasons, I had been in and out of college and in that season trying to figure out what on earth my life was about. *What are you going to do with me?* I knew I could not do a normal job. But I had no idea what anything else would look like because, for me, this is what you do. I never considered ministry. It never came into my mind. I was in this constant wrestle over, *God, what are you going to do with my life?*

Though externally things had really stabilized for a moment, I was still in that season where I was growing in watching and listening. The Holy Spirit was teaching and growing me in my gift. I had a situation that was a turning point for me with some things. It was the time I first knew of an encounter with the spirit of Jezebel.

I had met these people who were doing a home church. Of course, I was still going to my church as well, but I had just become friends with these other people who were starting off in ministry. I didn't know them very well, but a few months into just being friends with them, they invited me over to their home because they were having the kickoff of their church. They had a good-sized home where they were doing meetings with maybe twenty people. They asked me to come early to pray with them, maybe five of them.

We were in their kitchen, in prayer. This was the first time that I can remember that I went into this type of an open vision where I was in a trance as we were praying. I was aware of what was in the room, but I was in another place. I was seeing things that were going on in the family and in their little community, basically. I saw the husband being unfaithful. I saw several other things that were going on, such as manipulating and lying. It stunned me.

I was in this trance, and people knew I was in it. I couldn't speak. It was like I was aware of what was going on in the room, but I was caught up in this other place. After just watching things in the Spirit, I came out of it. In shock over what I saw, I didn't know what to say. I excused myself and went to the restroom.

As I walked into the restroom, a demon manifested to me and said, "This is my day." This demon was threatening me because I had seen the truth of what was really happening. At the time, I didn't really know about Jezebel. Now, after the fact, I look back and think, *that's clearly what that was.* But I came out of the restroom, and I sat down and started to just call it all out. I did not have communion with the Lord or a conversation with the Lord over what I saw or ask Him about the demon that manifested. I just reacted. I reacted to everything I saw in the trance and the demon manifesting to me. I walked back into the kitchen and said, "None of this going on in this house is from the Lord." I started to call out everything that I saw, and I walked out of the house.

After this, I started to have major demonic attack in my life. Grace lifted from me to live righteously. I started going out and partying with friends from work. I had some sexual encounters. I was drinking and partying for nine months straight. Every single night, I would cry to the Lord because I didn't want to be doing what I was doing, and my heart was broken. Yet, I couldn't stop myself from doing it. I'm not joking when I say I cried every single night. I cried out to God to help me. I cried out in repentance every single night, and then I would get up and just go do whatever I was going to do.

It was a sad nine months of going to work. I wouldn't go to church sometimes because it was shame that kept me out of church. I didn't not go to church because I walked away from the Lord; it was shame of what I was doing that kept me out of the church. I would say I was going half of the time.

Still, my heart was very connected to the Lord. Since my encounter with the Holy Spirit, I have never turned away from the Lord, in my heart. My heart was genuinely broken. This went on for nine months, and I had this incredible sense that the Lord was in it. I remember having a conversation with a friend at the time and saying, "This is where I'm at. This is what's going on, and I can't explain it, but the Lord is in this." And she said, "You're crazy. The Lord's not in you doing this. The Lord didn't drive you to do this." And I knew the Lord didn't drive me to do what I was doing, but, He was there. I didn't know how to explain it, at the time. There was just this overwhelming sense that, *Lord, You're in this. I don't understand it, and I'm sad because I don't want to be doing this.* But I felt His leadership.

It sounds like a contradiction because I was sad over what I was doing, but I sensed His presence and His leadership in it. Not understanding it is what broke my heart because I loved the Holy Spirit so much that how I was acting and what I was doing just broke my heart. I didn't have it in me to choose what was good. That's what was manifesting: *I couldn't choose what was good.* Holy Spirit was also revealing my heart, and It was criticism; it was judgment; It was self-righteousness in me, really, pointing the finger based on what I saw in the house with the Family months prior. Not consciously, but obviously subconsciously, that was what was in me: self-righteousness.

Nine months into that season after every day crying out, one day it lifted. The presence of God came and washed over me, and it was the re-emergence of grace. When His presence was just washing over me, it was His love. It was His kindness. As He was washing over me, He was just speaking over me, "I love you, not because of anything you do, not because of anything you do."

That was the message He was speaking to me. He was saying, "I love you because I love you. And my love for you doesn't change because of what you just did in the last nine months." I thought that because I was doing these things, the Lord didn't love me. Of course, He hates sin, yet He said, "I love you. My love for you doesn't change." It was freeing me. I'm loved not based on anything that I do.

I really came to a deeper revelation that it was by grace that I was able to not sin. It wasn't my own righteousness; it wasn't in my own strength and my own ability. All those years, I thought it was my choosing. I thought it was my power or my strength to do righteousness. I was proud of that. Subconsciously, that was my attitude. The Lord led me into that situation in that home where I encountered that demon. I reacted in self-righteousness and judgment against these people, which opened the door of the enemy to come into my life and wreak havoc in my life.

The Lord waited to show me that it was not based on me. *You're not kept by your own power.* It was a powerful revelation for me that it's by grace that I am able to *not* sin. He showed me that when grace was removed temporarily, this was what it looked like. You act. You go back to carnal ways and do carnal things, and you sin. When grace is present in my life, then I don't sin. Obviously, we have to choose grace and receive it, and we must have hearts that want to obey. In my case, I wanted to obey, but I just did not have the power to obey because grace was removed for a moment. This was done to show me my need for grace and the power of it. The Lord was saying to me, "Regardless of what you did these last few months, I love you." That was stunning to me. I thought I had to pay for it or that I was a bad girl and there should be punishment for me, and He said, "Nope, it's gone, right now."

He showed me that He was the Father who loved me no matter what I did. He was consistent in love. It was a powerful revelation for me, and it set me straight on my course again. It lit me up even more.

When I was in the situation with the demon, I didn't put the pieces together yet, that God loved these people too. I still had this self-righteous, critical spirit that they were doing it on purpose just like I had been intentionally partying and living in unrighteousness. It was that judgment that I judged them with that I brought on myself.

Matthew 7:1 says, *"Judge not lest you be judged, because with the same judgment you judge, you will be judged."* And that's the situation that was happening to me. That's what I came under. I saw truth; I saw something accurately, yet I moved in judgment and in a wrong spirit. I moved in a self-righteous and critical spirit. I never had God's heart or God's mind in the situation, even though it was an accurate revelation. Because of that, I opened myself up to the enemy for that same judgment to come on me, and that's what I was in for for nine months. As I came out of that season I moved forward with a fresh love for the Father and for the Holy Spirit. I was grateful for the correction that the Lord had brought me into and even more grateful for the amazing revelation of His heart for me and for other people. I feel like prophetic people can be saved from so much trouble. Understanding this truth, when you see something that does not align with God, do not be so quick to make a judgment about it. Remember you also are weak and imperfect, so extend mercy and grace to people while they are in process. You would certainly want mercy from people if you were knowingly or unknowingly in sin, or just acting out of your weakness. James 2:3 warns us about this:

"For judgment is without mercy to the one who has shown no mercy. Mercy triumphs over judgment."

Prophetic people are not exempt from this truth just because they know or see something about someone. Personally, I believe when prophetic people move in judgment without mercy it is even more grievous to the Holy Spirit because you are claiming to speak in His name. He is jealous for His name, and His name is Mercy.

Even though I had come into this place of renewed love and restoration from those past nine months, I still had that underlying disruption about my life and who I was and what God was going to do with my life. At the time I was working a lot. I had a good job, but I was working a lot, and my daughter was at an age where she just really needed her mom as she was getting into those pre-teen years. It was a real struggle for me of wanting to be a good mom and having to take care of my daughter by working all the time. I had a survival mentality, a work mentality. No one had ever taken care of me. For the most part, my whole life, I was taking care of myself. And I didn't know it at the time, but inside of me it was, *I've got to take care of me, and I've got to take care of my daughter because no one else is going to do it.*

I was a very hard worker. I had a good day job, and then I was working at night. At this time, I really started fasting and learning about fasting. I loved prayer and being with the Lord in the place of prayer. I had a nice, big walk-in closet that I cleaned out and I was going to go on a fast, so I was creating a prayer room in my walk-in closet.

I started this fast, and I was crying out to God that I wanted to be a good mom and be there for my daughter. I remember distinctly saying to the Lord, "I don't know what You're going to do with my life. I don't know what You could possibly do with my life." Being in and out of mental institutions, being in and out of school, I got a high school diploma. I was in and out of college and had no clue what to do with my life. I wanted to be there for my daughter, yet here was this issue that I needed to provide. The only thing that looked like to me was working hard.

Disturbed, I said to God, "I know You love my daughter more than I do, and You care about me being a good mom more than I do. I don't know what You can do, but You're God. Anything is possible with You, and I believe You. Do something because I really want to be with my daughter, and I want to be a good mom." I just cried out and believed He cared. I believed He was able even though I couldn't see a way through in the natural. My heart was postured in a way that I couldn't see what God could possibly do. I couldn't see it, yet my focus wasn't so much on the situation. My focus was on who God was. My focus was on, "You're God, and anything is possible with You. You spoke, and the worlds were created. Everything was created by Your mouth."

That's what my meditation was. "You created all things; all things exist by Your power. This isn't hard for You, and I believe You. I believe that's who You are, yet I don't know what to do. I can't see it. But this is who You are, and I believe You." It was simple faith.

I got up not really getting anything from Him. A few days later I was back in my prayer closet worshiping the Lord, and He spoke to me. He said, "Quit your job." This happened all within a three-week timeframe. I knew He was continuing the conversation I had with Him a few days before, and I had a moment that was scary because in the natural, my life could all fall apart again. I had that happen many times already. I was homeless, and I had built things up to where we were doing well financially. It would be risky to quit my job.

I postured my heart like Esther where she said, "If I perish, I perish", and the heart posture of Daniel when He was told He had to bow before another god, and He said, "I am not going to bow to your god." He said, "My God will save me, but if He doesn't, I'm not bowing." I decided that I would err on the side of faith and take the

70

risk. I believed that He knew my heart.

I said to Him, "God, You know my heart. I don't know; I don't have the answer. I'm not one hundred percent sure that this is You. But I want to follow You, and You'll save me. But if You don't, I'm not going to trust in what I see. I'm not going to trust in my way. I'm going to err on the side of believing You, and if I perish, I perish."

That very day, I put in my notice for work. A week went by. I was in my prayer closet again, worshiping, and I had a vision of this area in Orlando where there are a bunch of stores. The Holy Spirit nudged me. He said, "Go there. Go walk down there." So, I did. I got up, and I went down to that area. I was walking around not knowing what I was doing there, and I came across a Christian bookstore that was fully stocked. It was closed, and it had a "For Sale" sign in the window. It was fully stocked: books, CDs, T-shirts, everything.

The Holy Spirit nudged me again, "Call the number." I said, "I don't have the money to buy a bookstore." I had just quit my job, and it made no sense to me. However, I had come to the point where I knew I was in this place with Him where there was no going back. You don't jump off the roller-coaster when it's in movement.

I called the number and said, "How much?" I asked the man, "How much are you asking for the bookstore?" He said, "Well, it belonged to a pastor's wife, and she went MIA nine months ago and basically forfeited everything. So, make me an offer." I said, "Well, approximately how much do you want?" He said, "I told you. Make me an offer." I said, "Okay, I'll call you back."

I have always loved books, and I had boxes and boxes and

boxes of books. There were books all over my apartment. The Lord had spoken to me probably six months before this to get rid of all my books that I had. I mean, you could take everything, but just don't take my books. Have whatever you want, but don't take my books.

When He said, "Get rid of your books." It was so difficult for my heart. To get rid of one book was tearing my heart, but I did. I listened to Him, and I started giving away my books. I had so many books that it was hard to find new homes for all of them. What's funny is, during that same season, as I was just getting rid of these books, my daughter and I were talking in the car one day when it randomly came up. I said, "Wouldn't it be fun to have a Christian bookstore? That would be fun." It was just a short conversation. I never prayed, never asked for it.

Now here I was talking to a man about buying a bookstore, however, I did not have money to buy a bookstore! The guy said to me, "Make me an offer." I went back home into my prayer closet and said, "God, here I am, what are we going to do?" I always had a really good work ethic. My dad owned businesses, and I believed that I had a little sense of honorability and respectfulness. I didn't want to have this guy in conversation with me, and I didn't even have the money to give him. That was a wrestle for me with the Lord. I really didn't understand at that point how God's ways seem so foolish to men, and that He was looking for faith. He was looking for someone to believe Him. He was looking for someone through whom He could show Himself strong. He wanted a carrier of the testimony of who He is. And He wanted to be gracious to me.

I said, "Lord, what on earth are we doing?" And I said, "You know, he was telling me to make him an offer. What do I offer him when I don't even have the money?" And the Lord spoke to me and said, "Offer him $100.00." I thought, "How on earth am I going to do this? That is so disrespectful to offer this man $100.00. You just don't do that."

Yet, again, I was in this moment of following the Lord. I was in this holy moment of just trust and faith. The Lord was doing something, and I had to stay on this crazy train, so to speak. So, I called the guy again, and I said, "Hi, it's me again. I'm just, again, asking how much you want for the bookstore." And he said, "I told you. Make me an offer." So, I kind of chuckled to sort of blow it off, you know, that I was being funny and not serious. I said, "Okay, $100.00 then." And he said, "It's yours."

I was stunned. I met with the guy the next day. He gave me the keys to the bookstore, and I'll never forget opening that door to that bookstore and sitting there and crying. I was realizing in such a deep, deep way the heart of God. God is looking for people to believe Him. Things don't need to make sense if we just trust Him. If we just follow His voice, even when we're not one hundred percent sure whether it's His voice or not, it's the heart posture. We are not being presumptuous but really believing, "I think this is You. And God, You know my heart, and I'm going to follow You. And if I'm wrong, I'm Yours. You'll save me. But if not, I'm going to go for it."

This situation laid a powerful foundation for me in my walk with God, who He is, and what He seeks. It laid a new foundation of faith and of trusting His voice. Over these years He was rooting me deeper and deeper in following and trusting His voice, not trusting in what I see in natural circumstances, but His voice. I believe that any person called to be a prophetic voice will go through these "risky" type of situations. It is invaluable in being established in knowing Him and His voice. Receiving the bookstore started a completely different journey for me where my daughter was able to come and work with me.

Having the bookstore was a sigh of relief to some degree because I'd always had that entrepreneurial spirit. When I was working as a psychic, I was working for myself. I was teaching classes at different places. I had my own clients where I was building and creating something. That was who I always was. Coming into the bookstore, it was me being able to move into that entrepreneurial spirit again which gave me levels of real satisfaction. Being able to not have to work when I chose not to, and work to provide for my daughter was a blessing.

At that time in my life, I was so hungry for more of the Lord and wanting to really grow and help people. I had an opportunity where I was able to work with a private foster care agency who took in children that the state could no longer keep for different reasons. I trained and took classes to become a foster parent and be licensed with this agency for special needs children. I took in teenage girls who were on a lot of medication with emotional and mental issues that the state would not take. My heart understood their journey somewhat. Even though I had never been a foster child, I knew abandonment, and these girls definitely felt abandoned.

I also somewhat understood the system because I was in and out of mental institutions and off and on medications. I wanted to love these girls, and I wanted them to know the Lord. I wanted my daughter to begin loving and helping people and reaching out, as well. So, we started to take in these girls. There would be between two to four girls at a time, usually anywhere from ages fifteen to eighteen. It was quite a difficult journey. I had my car scratched up and my house set on fire. I realized that to these girls, love looks like pain, so you love them the best that you can. They'd get close to you, and then they would lash out at you just from fear of an automatic response that *you're going to hurt me, so I'm going to hurt you before you can hurt me.* That was their way of keeping me out.

In this place I recognized my barrenness once again, I would go to the Lord and say, "Lord, I'm empty right here. I need you to fill me up with your love because right now I don't want to do this anymore. I need to be filled with your love." It was where I started to really cry out more and more for the love of God to fill me. The cry of my heart was for His heart. These girls went to church; they got saved. I led many of them to the Lord but didn't really see a lot of fruit. Years later, I got a letter from one of the girls who said, "I want you to know you changed my life. You loved me so well." Of course, at the time, I didn't experience any of that or see any of the fruit of it, but I know that those seeds were sowed, and it was such a blessing to know that years later she was walking with the Lord.

I did that for a little over a year. It was a time for me of crying out for more of His heart. I knew I needed more of His love to be able to love back, but honestly it was the Holy Spirit leading me into these situations to expand my heart by once again bringing me face to face with the barrenness on my heart. While caring for these girls, all they did was push me away, but Holy Spirit was saying to me, "Love them." I was constantly crying out for His love to fill me so that I could love these girls well. This cry to know more of His heart was consistent in my life since going through the situation with the house church. I was in "Holy Spirit School" in regard to my heart. He was wanting to move me forward into who I was called to be, and for these few years it had everything to do with how I was responding to what I saw in the spirit, and how I was loving people in different situations. I think that process never ends in our lives. We will always have situations to grow in our love for God and people. In this particular season I was in an intentional season instigated by God to expand my heart to love. I never could have been trusted with more of the Word of the Lord without knowing and having His heart. For me, this is the way He chose to bring me into this reality. I know it is not the same for everyone, BUT if you are called as a prophetic voice, you will be confronted with these tests. God wants us all to grow in love, but as a prophetic voice these tests are essential to grow in stewarding the Word of the Lord. Loving abandoned teenage girls may not have looked like it had anything to do with my prophetic journey, but wow, was it ever such a huge part of it! Sometimes we think that when we cry out for something, like His heart or His love, we're just going to have the Holy Spirit come and give it to us. Sometimes He does. I've had those times as well. But, most of the time, it comes in ways we don't even recognize.

With my church, at the time, I was moving in prophecy and would get encouraging words for the church. I loved prayer. One day I was in prayer with the Lord, and He took me into an encounter like He did with Ezekiel, literally by the hair in the Spirit over an organization, He took me room by room, and He showed me different things that were occurring. He showed me man's plans and man's agenda. He showed me even where someone was being unfaithful in their marriage. Automatically, after this encounter of the Lord showing me all this, I said, "I'm not speaking a word" because I remembered when I had something similar happen back with the house church and what happened to me. This time I said, "I am not speaking a word," because I was not going to have all hell break loose again. I was in self-preservation mode.

I went to bed that night, and I had a dream. In the dream, the leader of the organization was pointing at me from a platform, and he said, "Speak." I woke up from the dream and thought, "Okay, God, you want me to speak." I didn't understand it, but I went with it. This time I didn't say anything, but I wrote it all down and gave it to the leader.

It didn't go over very well. It was rejected. I thought again, "God, why am I here again? What is going on? I do Your Word. I say Your Word. I respond to what You show me. You spoke to me in the dream to speak, and I spoke. Then it's like hell breaks loose again."

Once again, I realized that even though I was having visions that were accurate and true and that the Lord led me into them, I still responded without having His counsel. At the time I didn't even realize that I needed to ask him about what I was seeing. I thought that because I saw it, I should say it. But all the while I was seeing accurately and then responding from my soul, my interpretation. I had not yet learned that not only did I need His love in my heart, I needed His counsel. The letter I wrote to the leader was a far better response than how I responded with the house church situation, but it was still so off. And, this was all the Lord's doing. It was Him leading and teaching me. The Lord brought me into that situation where I saw Jezebel and came face to face with that demon. The Lord brought me into the encounter where He took me by my hair over the organization and showed me what was happening. The Lord spoke to me in the dream to 'speak.' The Lord gave me these tests to bring me into seeing what I lacked, and He brought me into correction. He was teaching me. He was growing me.

I once again realized, "Oh, I need God's heart on the matter." I was seeing something accurately, yet I didn't have His perspective about it. I didn't have this language at the time, but now I see so many people have encounters. They have accurate revelation. They have visions. They're seeing accurately, yet especially as seers because seers see, they'll have encounters and see things accurately and not have the Lord's perspective over it. It hurts so many people.

We see this in the prophets with Ezekiel and Jeremiah. The Lord would bring them into seeing something, and the Lord would say, "What do you see?" Then there would be communion back and forth that would be conversation where they would get the Lord's perspective. For me, at the time I was not doing that. I was having the visions, I was having the encounters, and I was reacting. I didn't understand yet. I didn't know how to do that. I went from one extreme of just reacting and judging and criticizing to the other where I would not speak at all. Then when the Lord told me to speak, I still moved in a measure of judgment and criticism and pointing the finger. It was not the heart of God.

That was a major moment for me of realizing that I didn't know how to do that, and I didn't understand what I needed to do because I had no training in the prophetic. This was all the Holy Spirit, for several years up to this point, taking me into situations. It was rough. I stumbled and hit my head and fell into sin, made people mad, experienced rejection, etc. This training with the Holy Spirit and revealing what was in my heart was such a painful process that I did not understand any of it until after the fact. After the fact I would then say, "Oh" and "This one was life changing for me" or "Wow, I need to understand the Lord's heart. I need to have the Lord's heart." I would later come to understand that walking through these things would be more than essential for the next place He was bringing me to.

GO TO KANSAS CITY

I did have measures of breakthrough in my heart with the girls. But going through the season of really recognizing my lack of the love of God and just trying to be filled with more of it led me into fasting and praying. It was the Holy Spirit who was giving me hunger to move more into that love. I was on a fast and came to Mathew 7:21 where Jesus says, *"Not everyone who says to Me, 'Lord, Lord,' shall enter the Kingdom of heaven, but he who does the will of My Father in heaven. Many will say to me in that day, 'Lord, Lord, have we not prophesied in Your name, cast out demons in Your name, and done many wonders in Your name?' And then I will declare to them, 'I never knew you; depart from Me, you who practice lawlessness!"*

It's one of those moments where you're reading the Word and your heart is gripped with a Scripture. This was one of those moments for me where the words, *I never knew you*, gripped me…and that this was Jesus talking. This term*, to know*, means as a man knows a woman. It's Jesus saying, *I never knew you as a man knows a woman. You never knew me as a woman knows a man.* I was caught up in this moment where I had to be honest in my heart about Jesus.

I was confronted with the truth, and said, "Jesus. I am not in love with you." Now, I believed in Jesus. I was grateful for Jesus. I accepted Him as my Lord and Savior. I believed in Him. But when it came to this Scripture, the reality was, I was not in love with Jesus like a woman would be with her husband. I didn't have that kind of love; and it was disturbing.

I found myself weeping and weeping and weeping like, "Wow." For me, up until this point, the love of the Father and of Holy Spirit was the revelation of my life. But this time, Holy Spirit, the Spirit of Truth, had broken into my life and was showing me Jesus in a new way. I was always very aware of the revelation of the Father. The revelation for me was that I was His little girl. I was delighted in my Father in heaven. That was something that I lived in every single day. *I have a Father in heaven, and I'm His little girl. He treasures and loves me. I have this safe Father.*

He was my safe Father, and I lived in that place. So, this was a new introduction for me, believe it or not. And this was eight years into being a Christian. I realized that though I loved God the Father and the Holy Spirit, I didn't really know Jesus. I didn't love Jesus the way that this Scripture was speaking to me, and it terrified me in a good way. It was the fear of the Lord.

I cried out, "Jesus. I don't love you like this, and whatever

You need to do in my life to bring me into this, do it." Little did I know what that prayer would do to my life. You know those moments in your life where you look back and say, *that changed my life forever*? Sitting on my living room floor with my Bible open reading Matthew 7:21 and having the Spirit of Truth touch my heart would not only forever change my life but set the course for the rest of my life. I can look back now and say that moment was one of the most important moments of my life.

Probably a week later in prayer I heard the Holy Spirit whisper to me, "Kansas City, Missouri, pack your things." He was calling me to a ministry there. I knew it was the Lord's voice once again leading me.

I responded immediately. I started the process of selling the bookstore, liquidating it, getting everything in order, and selling my things. I went online and signed up myself and my daughter for an internship there at the ministry. With the money I received from selling the bookstore, I paid for our apartment for two months as well as the internship that my daughter and I were going to do.

That whole summer my daughter and I planned to go up earlier before the internship, but my mom ended up passing away that summer. It caused quite a bump in the journey. It was a sudden death, and my heart went into a really dark place. My mom's passing, along with some other things, threw me into a lot of warfare before going to Kansas City. There were a lot of challenges, which more came from the state of my heart at the time.

Two days before my daughter and I were planning to leave, the Holy Spirit spoke to me about emptying my bank account. He asked me to give it all to an orphanage in Haiti. I was stunned and excited at the same time. He created me to love adventure, and this was certainly an adventure He was inviting me to. The idea of trusting Him this way was exhilarating. I had no issue emptying my account because I thought that if He was asking me to give it, that He would certainly give it back to me. I can still see myself sitting there staring at that send button, saying, "Here we go, Jesus."

Chapter 6

Falling in love

Responding to the invitation to "know Him."

I arrived in Kansas City with my daughter, Kasey, in the middle of the night. Not knowing what to expect from this new town, I looked around and began to cry. I was devastated because it was clearly not a good neighborhood. I was used to a nice house in a clean environment with a nice neighborhood. Here I was following God into a place where I did not feel safe; it was very old, very run-down. As I cried in the parking lot, I said to God, "You brought me to this." At that point, because of all the warfare I had experienced for several months prior to this, like my mom dying, I had no desire, no excitement. It was pure obedience. I went because I knew God had spoken. I felt, at the time, I was like the walking dead. I had no emotion, and my past was gone. I didn't know what to expect for my future. I was numb. But I knew it was from God; that was the only reason I went. I had to go forward.

Starting the internship was quite a shock for me. The Word was being opened to me in a way it never had before. About a month into the internship, one of the leaders in the prophetic department in the ministry that my daughter and I got connected with allowed me an open door into the prophetic department. So, before I was even out of the internship, I was on the prophecy teams and a part of the dream department, I also ended up being an assistant to the man that led the dream interpretation department. He was teaching weekly classes and leading seminars and was a leader in the prophetic department. The Lord moved my heart to serve him and his wife and family. The Lord gave me that assignment to see how I could help his wife as she was raising small children, so I did that with all my heart.

I understand now that Gods brings us forth into leadership positions through serving. A heart that wants to serve and serves well is a heart prepared to lead. Leadership, at the end of the day, really is being a servant to the people you are leading. I did not know God was preparing me to step into leadership.

About two months into the internship, I was really feeling the pressure that month three was coming up, and I had to pay rent. I didn't know from where the money was going to come. There was a dear couple in Orlando supporting us at the time, but it wouldn't be enough to cover everything that we needed. Growing up fiercely independent, a single mom and never really being taken care of from a young age and in and out of mental institutions, I learned to take care of myself. I was about to discover how much I still believed that it was up to me and that I was responsible for myself even after all God had done in my life so far. With that third month coming up, I began to feel the pressure, and I had to do something. Accusation and offense against God was coming up in my heart. I expected Him to take care of me. I trusted Him, I had the money, and gave it up. I believed it was a simple transaction: when I give, He gives it back. When I didn't see that happen as I thought it should, my sense of entitlement and offense and anger manifested toward God. Month three came, and there was no breakthrough. We got into the middle of month three, without the rent paid, and the fire was on. When I was a few weeks late on the rent, they called me into the office and said, "The leadership here says to everyone that if they can't pay their bills, they need to get a job." That was music to my ears because I wanted to get a job. I imagined that I could go and be a waitress in a nice place and make money quickly to solve this "problem." That was my temptation in that season because I was hearing from the Lord to not get a job. I found myself once again in this place —*do I trust what I believe I'm hearing from God or go take care of myself?*

I was glad to hear them suggest a job because it seemed like permission from my leadership. I had the green light. Being used to self-sufficiency, and with my anger toward my assumption that God wasn't taking care of me, I put out applications and set up appointments. I'll never forget that day. It was the spring. I was sitting outside a coffee shop and I had a one o'clock appointment for an interview. I remember looking at the clock at 12:30, and I had the strangest sensation. I was frozen there; I was unable to get up from the chair. I could not seem to move. I thought, *there goes that job.* At 1:15 my phone rang. It was the apartment complex office calling. A day prior, I had received a three-day notice of eviction from the apartment, so when I was getting a phone call from them, I didn't answer it. However, I knew I had to go back to my apartment and talk to them. In that moment I wondered if I had really heard God. I remember saying to Him: *God, I am yours. You know my heart. I want to follow You and Your voice. I believe You spoke to me. You are God. What You decide to do with me is up to You. If I end up on the streets, I still have you. But my heart has been true and I decided to trust you.* I went into the apartment complex, and they informed me that someone came in and paid my debt and paid the next month as well. It just broke me.

That experience shifted my life because the other part of this story is that the Lord was teaching me, *I don't want you to do faith by suggestion, saying you're going to trust me while telling everyone else what you need, hoping they rescue you.* That was a big part of this: just me and God and me not telling everybody. I really did that. I only asked one person to pray with me. They encouraged me to keep going. Nobody knew. When someone showed up to pay my debt and the month ahead, it showed me again who God is and that I could trust Him. He provides. I realized that God was wanting me to see who He really was. If He had shown up early, there wouldn't have been that fire that revealed offense, expectation, entitlement, anger, or the fact that I thought it was just a simple transaction. It was much more about the discovery of who He is and that He is trustworthy, but not on my terms, on His terms. It was a beautiful breakthrough for me of seeing Him even more as the One who leads. I can surrender what I think and trust Him to lead me.

WHAT IS PROPHECY

That breakthrough inside me and with my finances completely shifted things. I did not lack in my finances from then going forward. I was not prospering, but my needs were met. It was like that manna, that daily manna from Heaven that I had exactly what I needed. At this point I was on staff full time in the ministry. I also spent several hours a day in the local prayer room. My life was the prophetic ministry, fasting, and being in the Word.

It was a time of richly growing in the Word. I would say several months into this, maybe the year mark of my arrival there, I started to get really disturbed inside. It was a Holy Spirit confrontation. I was asking the question: *Lord, what is the difference between what I used to do as a psychic and what I am now doing in the prophecy rooms?* In the past I would meet people and tell them what I would see. I was doing the same thing in the prophecy rooms: telling people what I would see. I was very aware that the Spirit by which I was functioning was different. But I still wondered *why* we were doing this. *Why do I just sit in front of someone and give them information, read their mail?*

Over the years I had grown in the prophetic, and I grew in the Lord's heart. At this point in my immaturity, I was still stumbling a bit in getting His counsel with things that I saw; I knew that He wanted people to know His mind and heart. But I had this sense that there was something that I was missing. *Why? Why do we prophesy?* There was a deeper understanding that He was inviting me into. I did a lot of fasting and searching out the Word to answer that 'why' question. *What is prophecy about?*

The first place I started, which obviously is the most common place, was 1 Corinthians 12. Prophecy is for edification, and exhortation. But then I would ask what does exhortation really mean? What does it mean to edify? What does it actually mean to encourage? But the Holy Spirit was wanting to lead me in a different direction with it. He led me to Revelation 19: *"For the testimony of*

Jesus is the spirit of prophecy." That Scripture lit my world on fire. Jesus has a testimony. So, what is Jesus' testimony? Like going into court and giving a testimony, it's the truth about something. This led me on a journey of, *what is the testimony of Jesus?* I discovered that Jesus has a testimony, and it is about His Father.

He, the Word of God sent to earth, is the exact representation and image of His Father. His life and being is the image of the uncreated God. When we see Jesus, we see the Father. Therefore, Jesus' very life is a prophecy about the Father. The deepest passion about Jesus' heart was not first about us, but about a great passion and deep love for His Father. Revelation 19:10 was an opening up to me that it was about the Father. Jesus, through His life, words, nature, and heart, is a representation of how far the Father went to bring us into seeing Him. He so longed for us to see who He really is that He sent the Word to earth. Jesus is a cry from the Father, an expression of the Father that we would know who He really is. This just blew my mind because it was the starting point for prophecy.

Again, I was asking *why prophecy?* When we think of it, we put it in a little box like it's giving us information or telling us our identity. That is a part of the purpose and reason that prophecy exists but not the heart of it. That's just a small sliver of the reason prophecy even exists. He really started to bring me into understanding that this is the passion of Jesus. I was introduced to the revelation of Holy Spirit's role in prophecy. He's actually the Spirit of Truth. Jesus speaks of this in John 16:14 regarding Holy Spirit. He says, *"...He will take of what is Mine and declare it to you."*

The Holy Spirit is the Revealer, and His primary job is to

reveal the testimony of Jesus. The Holy Spirit is the spirit of prophecy. He is the witness. Jesus has a testimony, but Holy Spirit testifies. It brought me into this whole revelation of the foundational truth about prophecy: it is about revealing God. It is not only His mind and heart but even more importantly WHO He is, His nature. I was in Isaiah 40 for several months. My eyes were opened to see things I had never seen, not only in Isaiah 40 but the Word in general. I saw the cry of God's heart for us to behold, to see, to behold Him.

The heart of the prophetic is to bring people into seeing and beholding God and to truly know him, intimately.

During this time and from this revelation, Holy Spirit birthed the prophetic teachings that would be foundational for the ministry I would walk into later.

INVITATION

My time in Kansas City would begin a journey to depths of surrender that I couldn't have imagined. Of course, I didn't know that at the time. I didn't know it was surrender He was looking for in me. There was a lot of undoing, revelation, fasting, emptying and crying. One day in the prayer room Jesus spoke these words to me: "Will you give up your justice?" I knew what He meant without Him saying anything more. *It is fascinating how when He speaks it's like volumes of information with one word.*

Growing up with everything that had happened to me, I had such a sense of injustice. I couldn't think of anything good that had ever happened to me until I came to the Lord. It was one traumatic event after another until I came to know the Lord. When I looked back on the past, I just saw injustice. I thought that coming to the Lord would give me justice. I thought that He would repay for all that had happened to me. Following the Lord, I always had a 'yes' in my heart. When He spoke to me and invited me to do something, I always had an immediate yes. I couldn't remember a time I had said no to the Lord or struggled with a yes. This time when He came and asked me to give up my justice, I was traumatized. I was more traumatized because of the condition of my heart that I could not say yes to Him. I considered in the moment if this might be like an Abraham and Isaac moment. I certainly hoped that was the case, that maybe He was just testing my heart. I thought, *you're asking me to give up my justice, but you're not really going to withhold justice from me.* But I didn't know that for sure.

I didn't respond to Him right away. I went home and wept for days over the fact that I couldn't say yes to Him. A few days later I found my yes. I cried my way to the yes. I didn't understand it, but I was willing to trust Him and give up my justice. As I said yes to Him, I went into an encounter. I found myself at a gate, an ancient looking iron gate in a forest with Him on the other side of the gate. Behind Him the woods were very dark. It was cloudy and rainy, and I couldn't see into the forest. He was standing behind the gate, and He said, "Come with me." I knew that where He was inviting me was going to be difficult, but I opened the gate and I went to follow Him into the forest. As we went into the thick of the forest, I came out of the encounter. I would not understand until several years later what Jesus was inviting me to. He was answering my cry He gave me the day I sat before Matthew 7:21, to know Him and love Him.

I stepped into a role of helping to create a training arm for the prophetic department. My first class included around fifty people. From those people, I started teams for the evening section in the prayer room. People would come to town and sign up for prophecy in different time slots. I had thriving teams and was really enjoying what I was doing. I was coming alive in a new way. So many of the things that I had learned on my journey I was now being able to share with others. After some time, I was invited to step into more leadership in the prophetic department. I was helping to lead the department as well as teaching, training, and leading thriving prophetic teams and really growing in my prophetic gift as well as growing in leadership. My life was about being in the prayer room, in the place of prayer in the Word, and serving in the prophetic department for the first few years. I did begin to travel a bit, speaking and teaching all over the world. During that time, I really felt the Lord's hiddenness and jealousy over me. I had an overwhelming sense that He was intentionally doing something with my life, but I didn't have any idea what it was. I would have visions, and He would speak to me about who I was. I had constant visions of me being an eagle in the spirit with Him flying with me. He would speak to me about what it meant to be an eagle and that I was a mother of eagles. These were vague things that I didn't understand at the time, but I knew He was calling me to be a leader.

I felt His jealousy so much to an extent that I was so limited as to what I could do. I found a good little community, but I was limited in relationships, particularly romantic relationships, which was probably the most frustrating for me at the time. When I would have an opportunity to be in a relationship, He would shut it down every single time. This brought up offense and anger dealing with what I wanted versus what He wanted for me.

I would have a constant vision of myself while in prayer. I would see a situation with a dog in a yard where the owners maintained boundary lines for the dog. I was like that dog that would get past the lines. Of course, I'm not a dog, and God's nature is not controlling, but the vision would be like this. Because the dog was allowed to stay only in the yard, there were boundary lines. Like the dog, I would try to run out into the street, but an invisible electric fence would zap me if I got outside these invisible lines. In this vision, as I tried to stray, I would be zapped every time. The boundary lines represented something that I wanted outside of what His heart had for me, and when I would hit that boundary line something would sting me. It would hurt me emotionally or be a form of rejection. For years I had this vision, and I began to learn that He was teaching me to stay within these lines. Eventually, I began to see myself learning in these visions that I was a dog that was comfortable not trying to get out of the yard. I was at rest; I had found a peace. It symbolized me trying to fulfill myself outside of the things He had for me. When I tried to go outside those boundary lines and then get zapped, the pain I experienced started to shift me. At the time I didn't realize what was happening. It was a difficult process; it's a difficult process for all of us. I had to realize that it wasn't the Devil hurting me, it was me hurting me. We are told that Jesus learned obedience by the things he suffered, well guess what, so do we.

The Lord was teaching me how to rest in Him and be in the boundary lines that He set for me and to trust Him and the good things that He had for me. That played out a lot for me in the beginning years regarding personal and romantic relationships. However, it also played out in ministry context by trying to exert my opinion, give a word, or try to be somebody. I knew it was the Lord at the time. It would bring up an offense and an anger. It would bring up this *self* that He was after. As I said, it took several years for me to find that place of rest. It was a very narrow space that He created. I couldn't get away with anything. What I could do, say, who I could be with was very limited, but it taught me obedience and to trust Him even though I didn't believe it at the time. That experience helped form me because it killed my flesh in a big way. I am much more able now to discern boundary lines He has set for me, and I don't try to go outside those lines. I don't want to eat anything that He's not serving me which is more than enough. Even though in the beginning it seemed like a very narrow place, what I found was like Hosea 2. At the time, Hosea 2 and Song of Solomon were constant themes in my life about my journey. In Hosea 2, He says, "*I will lure her; I will bring her into the wilderness; I will hedge up her way with thorns.*" And it's a narrow, tight place with thorns. If you try to get out of that place, the thorns will prick you, but the promise there in Hosea is what I found.

He says, "*...but in that place is a door of hope.*" What I thought was a narrow place turned out to be a very wide place of hope when I gave up what I thought I wanted. This door opens, and He says, "*She will sing there.*" The promise of knowing Him in a certain way, *you will no longer look at Me this way; you will no* *longer run after your lover; you will no longer run after this; you will no longer run after that. All these things that you thought satisfied you, you will no longer run after them. You will remember Me, and you will know Me and will know that I am your husband. I am the One that provides for you; I'm the one that gives you this in season.*

That was the theme of my life for several years. Again, I was experiencing the promise of when I left Orlando to go to Kansas City. This was that Matthew 7 that pierced my heart that told me, *I don't know You Jesus, do whatever You need to do for me to know You.* That's what He was bringing me to, that Hosea 2 place where He hedged me in and said, *you're going to know Me here and know that I am your husband and that I provide for you.* He told me that it was a safe place to give up my life and surrender because I would find Him there and find how much He loves me. For me it was a discovery. It was finding Jesus as the Bridegroom God with fierce jealousy, intentionality and fire. I would hear this roar over me in the spirit, and hear Him say, *she's mine.* That roar had given me years of tears. I was encountering His jealousy that way and not understanding any of it at the time.

Chapter 7

The Cross

He has no form or comeliness; And when we see Him, there is no beauty that we should desire Him. He is despised and rejected by men, a man of sorrows and acquainted with grief. And we heard, as it were, our faces from him; he was despised, and we did not esteem Him.

My relationship with Jesus during these years grew exponentially. I spent hours in the prayer room devouring the Word, every day. I was in the place of prayer and just looking at Jesus. It sounds delightful, and it was, but it was also extremely hard. It was my dying place; it was where I went to die to myself. I had this sense again in my life that the Lord was being very intentional with me, being on this Song of Solomon journey. At first, I really resented it because it was so difficult. Dying is not fun; it's not easy. In that place I was encountering the Isaiah 53 Jesus. Then I came to a season where I couldn't do it anymore. In those years even when it was difficult, the presence of God was still so strong. I was having encounters in the Word and in visions. Then I came to this season where I just hit a wall. I'd come home and forget fasting: I'd be watching TV and eating Bonbons. I was in a season where I thought the presence of God was gone. It was devastating to me. But what I didn't realize was that Jesus was coming to me a different way, and I didn't recognize Him, so I thought He was not there. Of course, He had never left me. I remember it was Thanksgiving Day, and I was walking out of my bedroom. I heard His voice, and it stopped me in my tracks. He said, "Michelle. do you remember that boy in middle school who used to chase you around?" There was this boy who chased me everywhere; he really liked me. He was the kid that everyone made fun of who never took a shower and was just awkward; I was annoyed by Him. He was offensive to me. Jesus told me that He was that boy chasing me in my life right then. He was the Isaiah 53 Jesus. It stopped me cold in my tracks, and I fell to my knees weeping.

I didn't realize that He was bringing me to a place where I could meet Him at the cross. He wanted me to see Him, the broken One, who for a moment felt forsaken by His Father. I repented, and everything turned around for me that day when I opened myself up to His love that was coming to me in an offensive way. And it's so true, as Isaiah 53 says, He has no form that we would desire Him. When He comes to us in that form, we usually do not recognize Him because He is offensive to men and women. The cross is offensive to those who have not yet seen true beauty. The way we perceive beauty, love and kindness, as humans, is based on what feels good, and I wasn't feeling good. So, I couldn't see Him. After I repented, my eyes were opened, and I fell in love with the cross. It started a journey for me to head toward the cross, to encounter who He was there, and be willing to be there with Him. I found my greatest joy in the One who does not appear desirable. It's still like that in our lives. I see it in my own life now, and I see it in other people's lives. When He comes to us this way and invites us to meet Him there, to watch with Him, weep with Him, go to a place of suffering, we don't like it because it doesn't feel good. And yet that is where I have found the place of deepest intimacy. I would say that my relationship with Jesus, my love for Him, understanding of Him, relationship with Him went to whole new levels. This is the Song of Solomon 5 place of where I fell so much more in love with Him when I saw the bloody, bruised, beaten One. It started a different journey for me about who He is. Not only had I been seeing my Bridegroom, husband, but now I was seeing my husband on the cross who died. He was inviting me to give my life for Him, the way He had given His life for me. If you are a follower of Jesus, this is your story; and the cross is the central part in the story. Yes, I know how offensive that can sound, but this is the place where we make covenant with God. This is the place of the most glorious, beautiful love. Sacrifice. I believe so much of the body of Christ right now is not walking in the true gospel. So many are unknowingly living as carnal Christians. Carnal Christians are "self" focused. Everything revolves around how we feel, what we want, our dreams, our desires, etc. Jesus is longing for a bride who will love him back with the love He is worthy of. He defines love. He did define it at the cross. He gave all of himself at the cross. He invites us into the same thing. I believe many do not understand this or what it looks like. I believe individually and corporately we all at some point end up in the John 6:26- 71 place on our journey.

Here, the masses were following Jesus. They were following Him because they saw Him miraculously feed people and do amazing miracles. In short, they were following Him because of what He could do. Seeing all of these things they wanted to make Him king. They believed He was their Messiah because of what He was doing. Jesus, knowing this, stops dead in His tracks and offends their minds. He says something they do not understand. They cannot understand the words of the spirit. He speaks of eating His flesh and drinking His blood. The very ones that believed in Him and wanted to make Him king turned on Him and walked away. He then turns to His disciples and asks them, "Does this offend you?", "Do you also want to go away?" In us, he is looking for the same response as Peter had, "Where else would we go? You have the words of life." The disciples expressed that they also did not understand what He was saying, yet they pushed through the offense. When we don't understand what He is doing, or what His motive is we will not recognize Him when he comes to us in a new way. When many are presented with suffering or sacrifice, they cannot comprehend that it would be God. They think it must be the devil, or they try and figure out what they did wrong to be in the place they find themselves. Oftentimes it is God. He wants to offend our minds with things we don't understand, he wants to call us to places that don't make sense. He wants us to follow Him and trust Him. Just like Peter in this story, He is wanting to draw forth the yes in us despite what we see in the natural. He is bringing forth love in us. When we are in confusing situations will we get offended and walk away, or will we trust Him and push through what does not feel good?

Shortly after falling on my knees in repentance, I went into one of the most profound encounters I had ever had up to this point. A profound encounter I had at the cross really helped shape my perspective. It happened when I was driving in my car headed to a meeting. I had my radio on worshiping the Lord and adoring Him. Nothing else was on my mind. Suddenly, I heard His voice ask me a question. He said, "Michelle, what do you want?" When He asked me, I somehow knew exactly what He meant. He was referring to a romantic relationship. I was so aware in that moment that whatever I asked for, He was going to give me. I felt the presence of the fear of the Lord, there in the car. I knew that I needed to answer wisely. It threw me off because the question came out of nowhere. It wasn't something I'd been thinking or asking. As I pondered the question, I pulled the car over and responded to Him and said, "Lord, You know. You know my journey of love and what it's going to take for me to fully become that bride that you have called me to be. You know how to bring me forward in love. If that means You bringing someone into my life that has lots of issues and You ask me to love them through it or if that means You bring a man who has been through lots of healing, loves me and has capacity to love me the way that You do, You choose for me." My heart at that time was that it didn't matter to me the *way* that Jesus had for me. I knew that we're all on a journey of love, and all our stories are headed in the same direction. As the body of Christ, we are the bride being prepared to be ready for a wedding. He knew the way to make that happen in me. He's the potter; I'm the clay. He is the farmer; I am His land. He's my bridegroom; I'm His bride. He knows how to bring me forward in love. I was open to whatever that looked like. If it meant great challenges in a relationship with someone or it was easier, I was open to it. Immediately, when I responded to Him, I went into an encounter. I was standing there watching Jesus in the Garden of Gethsemane weeping. The only way I can explain it is like with the air when you walk into a room, you have a sense that something is going on in the room. It was the same way as I was watching Jesus in the Garden; I could feel the atmosphere in the air.

It was so pregnant with love. It was the love between a Son and a Father. I saw Jesus crying out to His Father with deep love and passion. I could feel the Father's love and passion for the Son and the Son's deep love and passion for His Father. I was watching the Son with His Father pour His heart out. It moved me to tears feeling the passion. There was so much love; I was in awe as I watched this, and there are no words for how it deeply touched me. The scene changed, and I was watching Jesus carrying the cross on the way to be crucified. Again, I was watching and aware of this identity of Jesus the Son. I kept hearing Holy Spirit say, "He did it the Father's way." Jesus was so committed to doing things the Father's way that it wasn't *His way,* and He did it for love.

He so desired to please the Father. Jesus didn't go to the cross or do what the Father was saying out of simple obedience. There was a trust that He had as a Son with His Father, and It was out of pure love and passion for the Father that Jesus did what He did. It was the love that He had for His Father that fueled the obedience. It was love itself that gave Him the strength to obey. I realized that obedience itself has no power to keep us long term. There was a power that we needed to obey the Word of God and obey what the Father was saying. I knew it was love. I was in awe watching it. As I was watching Him carry the cross, I was hearing the Holy Spirit say, "Christ, the wisdom of God" and so many Scriptures out of 1 Corinthians, Chapters 1 and 2. "Christ, the wisdom of God, the Father's way." It was so much understanding and volumes of revelation.

The ways of God seem foolish to men, yet they are wise.

The Father was putting His Son on a cross, and there was no greater wisdom. Jesus, the cross, is the wisdom of God. I was receiving downloads of revelation about the cross and the heart of the cross. The Father has wisdom and a way that looks foolish, and it looks like weakness. What a prophecy! The scene changed again. I was no longer seeing the Son and the Father, but Jesus was laying on the cross and looking at me as my Bridegroom. He was looking in my eyes and saying, "I did it for you." And in my heart, I was saying, "Yeah, yeah. I know." He said, "No, you don't get it. I did this for you. I did this so that all my Father has sown in you and created you for would come forth." When He was saying this, I was receiving so much impartation. As He was speaking, I could not contain the love that was coming at me, being imparted to me. It was waves of love washing over me. I remember thinking, "If I could just contain a pinch of this, it would be all I ever need." I was weeping and weeping under the tangible, honey love of God that was changing the molecular structure of my body. I could feel my body changing.

As He was saying this, I knew that I could never fail because He was fighting for me, and He was always fighting for me. He was the bridegroom that gave His life that we would have a way to come forward into all we are, and He was still fighting for me.

I remember thinking, "How could I ever fail?" That was profound. It imparted hope and courage to me. I could not get low enough to the ground during this encounter. He said, "I did this so my glory could be seen on you." It was blowing my mind, this reality. This is the Philippians 2 God that is so humble. I realized that He wanted me to be glorified. He wanted His glory to be seen on me. He wanted to crown me with glory, and I couldn't get low enough to the ground. You'd think with a statement like that, we'd be puffed up because it was all about me at that moment. But what it produced in me at that moment was a deep, *deep*, humility. His love received humbles us, it does not puff us up. What was coming out of my heart back to Him was, *I want to give You my life. I want to serve You. I want to see Your heart's desire get fulfilled. What can I do for You Jesus?* And He was speaking over me, *"I want you to shine. I want to serve you. I want you to be lifted up."* The response that came out of me was the same back to Him. *I want to give You my life.* This moment was like nothing I've ever experienced.

In this encounter where I was looking at Him as my bridegroom, He was declaring things over me and speaking things over me that were being imparted to me. There was this moment that He opened something up to me related to the mystery of Christ and the church. I was seeing Jesus as a husband but also the leader, shepherd, head, apostle, boss, CEO. He let me glimpse into this. The atmosphere was Ephesians 5, specifically 25: *Husbands, love your wives as Christ loved the church and died and gave Himself up for her.* I knew this is what Jesus had done. *And wives respect your husbands, giving them honor.* I knew that's what was happening between us in that moment. I had this understanding and revelation of how low He went to lift me up, and all I wanted to do was honor Him, give my life for Him, and see His desire fulfilled. As I glimpsed into the future, He showed me the structure of the church and the oppression of women and why Satan hates women so much.

Often in the church we have perceived women as a certain type of helpmate, helping the man's ministry be fulfilled. And yes, that is true. But there is so much more. Despite the perspective of the roles and the way we see the roles of men and women, He showed me the truth. I glimpsed into the future, and it blew my mind. I was thinking *this is going to bring a big shock to the world and the church* because the actual heart of Jesus is to see His bride rule and reign and to come into leadership with Him because women on earth are a prophetic picture of the bride of Christ. Jesus is not returning until He has that equally yoked bride ruling and reigning with Him. There's a co-laboring. The attempts of Satan to oppress women and keep them down has much less to do with women, but it's more about the promise to come for the church. I saw women rising in leadership and power with a strong voice in partnership with Jesus. I knew that in the process of that it would bring severe shockwaves to the earth and a realignment and a readjustment and that Jesus was intent on bringing justice to women. I remember saying, *wow, I'm not saying a word about this,* because I didn't want to appear as some kind of feminist. I remember saying to the Lord, "Don't send me to talk about this. Raise up men to talk about it." It was offensive because I was a single woman, and I didn't want to appear as a feminist or an angry woman who needed some kind of position of leadership.

I saw there would be a false movement of that arising again which was the pendulum swing of women being oppressed and Jesus coming to bring freedom. I knew there would be this extreme pendulum swing of women not being in balance. In the encounter it was the true heart of a woman that Jesus was calling out. It was so full of humility that she would give her life for her husband. There was this beautiful balance of a husband that would give his life for his bride, and his focus is her coming forward into all she is, just as Jesus does with us. Just as equally as he was doing that, so was the bride. Her focus was on his heart and how she could serve him and what she could do to see all that was in him and his heart come forward. There was this beautiful dance of humility and of giving each other's lives to each other.

I knew that was the true heart of Ephesians 5 and that Jesus was going to do it in the church. I saw the process of that coming forward was going to be painful, an adjustment, a realignment. I saw that there was a humbling of men coming from where they had oppressed women, and there would be a humbling of women if they tried to exert control or power or be disrespectful or dishonoring. I saw that there would be a false movement. The enemy always looks for opportunities to twist things. I saw in that moment that the enemy was waiting for opportunity to get his hand in the mix. He does not want the bride to come forward. I knew in looking at Jesus that He had already won, and there was no way I could ever fail or lose, and the Church was sure to come forward.

As I saw this was true in the expression of husbands and wives during this encounter, I was keenly aware of Jesus, the Apostle. He was showing me what true apostolic leadership looks like, as well as all leadership positions.

Chapter 8

Deeper love

*What things were gain to me, these I have counted loss for
Christ, yet indeed I also count all things loss for the
excellence of the knowledge of Christ.*

I had come to this place in my love for Jesus that had freed me of
the care of things, to a degree. Along with another person, I had this
opportunity to build the training arm for the prophetic department,
and we were having some disagreements over things. I didn't want
there to be contention, so I decided to step away. I knew he really
wanted to do this and really didn't want me doing it with him. I
went to my leader and explained that I needed to step away because
I didn't need the position or to be fighting with someone, so I knew
I needed to just let him do it. I had a lot of tests like that.

We had a big conference coming up which was always a
really busy time because I was under my leader overseeing and
administrating everything going on with the prophetic rooms. Jesus
had come to me and whispered, "Come with me." When He said
this, I saw myself in the Arizona desert. I knew He meant that I
needed to do it right away. It was this place of – *what do you do?* I
wasn't a flaky Christian. I had responsibilities and commitments. I
knew I had a choice. And I said to myself, *what do I love more?*
This is Jesus. He knows what He's doing.

I had a leader who understood, thankfully. I said, "If you have to fire me or find someone else, do it. But He's calling me, and I have to go." I didn't take my commitment lightly. This was a busy time, so it wasn't a light thing for me. I cared, yet I knew that I had to make a choice. Jesus was drawing me into deeper love with Him. Was my commitment to this greater than the call of Jesus to go? I made the decision that I would go whatever the consequences. This was a big part of what my journey looked like in those days: choice. What would I choose? My leader blessed me and said, "Go."

I immediately went home and packed a few things like a sleeping bag into my little SUV. I drove out into the middle of the Arizona desert and slept in my car for almost a week. In the middle of the desert, I cried out for Jesus like blind Bartimaeus. "Jesus don't pass me by. Open my eyes." There was a hunger that rose up in me to see the Man. It wasn't about feeling His presence. It wasn't about making me feel good, no. The Man had called me. He was waking me up and causing an even deeper hunger in me to reach for Him. Even though He had invited me, I knew He had invited me to cry out. I cried out for the Man. I longed to see the Man Jesus, and He came.

It marked my heart in several ways. In this place of choice and what I put value on, it doesn't mean we're flaky and just run off and whimsically say, "Jesus told me to do this!" I despise those things. I feel like they're irresponsible and not the nature of God. Yet at the same time, when it's really Him and really His voice— what do we choose? This is something that happens on a daily basis in how we live our lives, and He was working this in me in such a deep way at this time, living from this place of what I must daily choose. I must daily pick up my cross to follow Him. Daily, daily, daily. It was this inner place of where there were big choices with consequences, but He was working something in the state of my heart like a perspective of how to live my life from value. What was my main value? What did I love? What we love steers our lives. We will eat the fruit of what we love in our lives. Was my value more on this Man who was calling me or my job and reputation? Did I look weird, foolish, crazy, irresponsible in this decision? Or did I value His voice, call, and Him? Did I fear the consequences or what-ifs? What if I lost my job? I had come to this place in my heart where I was really falling in love with Jesus in a deeper way, and my value was the Man. It didn't matter what the cost was. This would be a consistent theme in a big way in my life in the next few years. It's a daily place that we live.

FALLING IN LOVE

This theme was burning in my heart in my prophetic teams and teaching about prophecy and really declaring that prophecy is about a Man. I burned for people to love Him. I knew that I had encountered something about Him in my journey and my relationship with Him. My life was becoming less and less important to me; what He wanted became of greater value. I was so passionate for people to love Him. I feel like I crossed a line. I stepped over to this other place where I had started off with ministry and opportunities and why I do what I do in my life. I would say I was doing it for Jesus and the Kingdom, and I truly believed I was. I didn't realize that it really wasn't true in my heart. Really, it was for me. I lived from a place and a perspective that though I believed I was doing it for Him, and in my heart, I meant it, I wasn't consciously aware of the fact that I was living for myself. I don't think any of us are until we're not anymore.

In a small way, I feel like I crossed over this line where I honestly didn't care anymore. I saw and realized something different. I had fallen in love to a certain degree to where my heart really was, *what do You want?* It wasn't about what I wanted anymore. I longed for people to love Him. I realized that that was the reason, not just for the prophetic but the reason—period. It is the reason why we're here. The Ephesians 4 reality of the offices (the apostle, the prophet, the teacher, the evangelist, the pastor) made me realize what that really mean, "And He Himself gave some to be apostles, some prophets, some evangelists, and some pastors and teachers, for the equipping of the saints for the work of ministry, for the edifying of the body of Christ, till we all come to the unity of the faith and of the knowledge of the Son of God, to a perfect man, to the measure of the stature of the fullness of Christ..." I tasted this revelation that everything is about this Man and what He is doing.

Everything was prophesying. Everything was about Him. We were here for Him. It was all this love story and this coming back to the Garden in a sense of communion with Him. And I touched His heart. I touched His desire and His longing for His bride. The longing of Jesus to satisfy His Father's heart and longing to be known and for a bride to know her Bridegroom. It wasn't just revelation, I had tasted it from His heart, from His perspective. It changed the way I did everything and the way I made decisions and lived my life. My heart was gripped with what He might want.

What will satisfy Your heart, Jesus? I realize, we do that to varying degrees; we go from glory to glory, from faith to faith, from love to deeper realms of love to falling in love with a Man if we give ourselves to that with that reality. One of my favorite things to gaze at is Paul in Philippians who had everything: stature, money, respect, position. He came from the best tribe. He was a distinguished man in his community who had it all. He said, *I count it as rubbish. It's nothing, but here's what I value: the excellent knowledge of a Man, Jesus Christ and Him crucified.* I believe I touched that same place that Paul touched where he was so in love with a Man that he considered everything else rubbish. Everything else meant nothing. Paul fell in love because he met the heart of a Man and saw the value of a Man, and everything he did was fueled by the love for a Man. To stay in the knowledge of this Man was a love relationship, and I tasted that. It shaped every single decision that I made and what I was teaching.

It answered so many questions that I had. I had found an answer to the *'why prophecy?'* question. It answered the questions of what I was doing, why He gifted me this way. It wasn't just to give people information about their future or say God loves you or share a little about God's mind and heart. That was all good, but it's small in comparison to the real reason for the prophetic, which was to bring people into a relationship. It was about bringing people to meet God and to cause people to turn their hearts to Him. I am not speaking of prophetically gifted people, but Prophets are messengers of the covenant first. True Prophets will burn for people to be in right relationship with God, to be aligned with God, because this is the filter they see through, God's burning heart for His people to know Him. You see this cry throughout the books of the prophets. God's cry through them was; Know Him, Love Him. It's different for evangelists. They burn with a passion for people to be saved. They burn for the souls of people. Prophets are the other side of the coin, they burn for the heart of God to be known and seen. All offices are so necessary for fullness, and everyone carries a different passion of the heart of God. There's a difference between 'we all can prophesy' and 'the office of a prophet,' but the same spirit, the Holy Spirit, who has a cry, works through them all. That is to return people to covenant with God, to walk with God, follow Him in covenant, to know His ways, and to walk in His ways. That question was answered through discovering the heart of Jesus and falling in love with Him. I was able to hear His heart. Through the prophets this cry is so obvious, but throughout the years I would really find myself weeping with God in the book of Malachi regarding His heart for the prophets.

Chapter 9

Come with Me

He leads us into storms and lands with giants, to show us who He is, so we can become who we already are.

After a few years of him forming the 'yes' in me in deeper ways, by choosing Him when given a choice with the small things in my life, He would now begin to bring my yes into even greater levels where it would impact my life even more and bring me more in love. I had come to a place in my life of living in great favor in my community, having a good reputation, and enjoying what I was doing. I was loving life in a good place.

After a few years of this, I then heard His sweet voice again. He was again extending me an invitation. He asked me if I would walk away from all of it. *Come with me*, He said. It was an invitation to leave my job, my community, my whole life and go to Africa and Israel for three months. I knew that He meant permanently walking away from my position in ministry. It was a stunning invitation because I had thought I would be there for the rest of my life. They were my people and my community, and I was growing in love and contentment. But I knew it was Him calling me. What could be my response? What else could I choose but His invitation? I said yes again to the adventure with Him. I went to my leaders and told them what I was hearing. They told me to go but encouraged me to not leave my position. Because I had several assistants at the time, my leaders encouraged me to put my assistants in place and just leave temporarily. They told me that having a ministry name backing me was important for me and that it would open doors for me. Oh, the temptation set before me of self-preservation, of having a reputation, a name, the backing of a well-known ministry. There are always voices encouraging us to do what God is saying in a slightly different way, a way that seems safer or where we would have more control, a way that makes more sense to the mind of man.

Satan tempted Jesus in the same way in the wilderness. He tempted Him with staying away from the narrow road that the Father was leading Him to and placed before Him an easier way. These voices sounded so good and made sense in the natural but opposed the Word that God was giving me. In the natural, what my leaders were saying made sense. Why would I walk away from having a ministry name backing me? That was only a test because I knew the Lord was calling me away. He wanted me to put my confidence in nothing but Him and Him alone. I told my leaders that there was no way I could do that because I knew the Lord had told me to permanently walk away. I had come to a place in my life where it was all about following His voice, and I knew His voice and when He was calling me. I believe it is so important to have counsel from the leaders in our lives, as God has given them charge over us. Yet, at the same time we cannot live off the words of other people, even our leaders. Since coming into the church, I always loved being submitted to a leader, it was such a safe place for me. Honestly, sometimes I tried to use it as an excuse not to do what God was telling me to do. Part of what the Lord was teaching me in this was about leadership, but also His leadership. It formed a big part of who I am as a prophetic voice and as a leader today. Especially as a prophetic voice. Our job is not to tell people what to do but to lead them to Christ. I love what Paul says in 1 Corinthians 4:14, *"Follow me, as I follow Christ."* Speaking as a leader; my job is not to tell people what to do with their lives, but to help them learn how to follow Jesus, and grow in hearing His voice for themselves. To learn to discern Jesus' voice and to be ok with them stumbling along the way. This is how we all grow in Him. I am not to replace the voice of God in anyone's life.

The questions were coming as far as what I was going to do afterwards. I didn't know that; I didn't have the answer. I simply knew that was what He was saying to me right then. He was inviting me into another leap of faith. Some would call this unwise, but I believe that way too many times we call self-preservation, wisdom. I always say that fears' favorite mask is wisdom. Fear is always speaking to us, it wants to keep us comfortable, safe. Unknowingly, we think it is wisdom, but ultimately it just makes us feel safe. Jesus is not interested in us feeling comfortable, he is interested in us coming forth into who we are and that only happens as we see him, follow him, and follow His voice. He is fearless, leaping on mountains. He is conqueror, and He invites us to run with Him, and be with Him where He is. If we listen to fear, we will never come into the fullness of who we are.

I began the process of putting leaders in place, selling everything, moving out of my house, and getting everything in order. I knew I was going for three months. I went to Israel and Africa, where I did a lot of ministering. In leaving Kansas City, my heart was exhilarated because I knew I was following Him, but there was a sadness because I was leaving what had become my family. There was an unknown; I really didn't know what I was stepping into. My time in Israel for six weeks had some ministry, but it was mainly just sitting with Him and weeping with Him. I had already taken several trips to Israel before. My time there was about weeping over the land with the Lord. The next six weeks we went to several places in Africa for ministry. Towards the end of the trip we left to go to South Africa and serve a ministry in Johannesburg. After that my plan was to go back to Florida. A ministry there had been asking me for over a year to come back home to Florida and build their prophetic department. So, the plan was to train their team and build their prophetic department, as well as travel the state of Florida helping other ministries do the same.

The ministry people in Johannesburg were so kind. Before we were to leave the country, the hosting couple invited us to take their car and go to Durban and enjoy the beach and relax for a few days at a place they had there. As we left the next day to head to Durban, my friend was driving the car. As we were waiting at a green light, my friend went to turn, and a small, speeding bus hit the side of the car where I was sitting. We spun around and hit a concrete wall. I lost consciousness. When I awoke, I couldn't remember where I was or what was happening. I recognized my friend. I was scared, and I could feel the spirit of fear in the car. I knew I couldn't come in agreement with that spirit. I closed my eyes and just said the name Jesus over and over. I knew I had to keep looking in His face. I went unconscious, but I awoke again by being cut out of the car. I was in and out of consciousness. They had strapped me down and put a brace on my neck. They had given me morphine on the way to the hospital. Little did they know I was allergic to morphine. It was a nightmare. No words can explain what morphine does to my body. I started screaming at the top of my lungs. Morphine gives me the opposite effect of what it does for most people. I was hysterical. I begged them to untie me and let me go. I couldn't move. They continued to argue that they didn't know if anything was broken. I screamed and screamed that I didn't care if anything was broken. I just wanted them to unstrap me, and I wanted to leave. They finally allowed me to sign myself out of the emergency room with my friend.

I found myself back in the hospital the next day. They admitted me, and I would be there for several days. The neurologist had nothing good to say about the state of my head. He would only tell me of the long-term effects that I would experience as a result of the accident. The doctor told me my brain needed to be at rest and have no activity. I was on anti-seizure medicine for mini-seizures. I was pleading with him to let me go home. I really did not want to hear the things he kept proclaiming over me regarding long term effects. I did not want to be affected by his words. After much arguing, he released me.

BACK TO FLORIDA

My daughter and I both went to Florida, and I immediately got to work. Up until this time, this was one of the most difficult seasons of my life. I was in and out of the hospital just about every week still having mini-strokes. I kept falling over. My adrenals were shot, but I just kept pushing myself. My daughter came under attack as this was happening to me. She had met some people, and I always say it was like the terrorists came and took my daughter away. I didn't know my daughter anymore. This guy came into our apartment and moved her stuff out. I just sat on the couch and cried. I felt like I couldn't keep my life together. I was trying so hard, and my daughter was taken from me. My worst fear had happened: that my daughter would not walk with the Lord. Some friends knew my situation, but I just felt so alone. I was building the prophetic department, training, putting leaders in place and traveling the state of Florida helping other churches and ministries with the prophetic and teaching in the prophetic, all while in and out of the hospital. I did that for seven months.

I finally just crashed and hit this point where I thought God had abandoned me. I had never felt anything like that to that degree. I knew in my mind He didn't. I didn't know at the time it was spiritual, but it was. It was a demonic attack. The enemy was taking advantage of me and my daughter in a vulnerable situation. After nine months of being in Orlando doing that, a leader in Kansas City who was very worried about me told me I needed to come back. It was hard; I had to leave my daughter who wasn't even talking to me. But I knew I had to get back to my community and in a safe place. I didn't make it back to Kansas City before I had to stop in Columbia, Missouri at an emergency room. My body was not doing well. When I finally got to Kansas City, I rented a basement apartment. I had been there for a few weeks when I had a dream one night that I was laying hands on someone and had gotten a word of knowledge for them. I wasn't looking at the person, but I looked over as I laid my hand on them. I saw that it was me that I was praying for. I woke up and was completely healed. I had not gotten another headache; every single symptom of the injury was gone. I spent several months after that spending time with the Lord just letting my body and soul rest.

Being back in Kansas City, I rested a lot. The previous year had felt like a non-stop boxing ring. I needed a breather. I learned so much from that season. The car accident was a demonic attack that affected my body in significant ways. I didn't steward that situation well at all; I just pushed through, ignoring a lot of things because of "the call." During my time building in Orlando, I kept pushing. I was in an interesting paradox. All that I was doing was really anointed; I had reached places in glory that I hadn't been to before. But I was the weakest I had ever been, and this was a different kind of warfare that I hadn't experienced before. I was swirling.

The weakness that I was in brought up deep, deep feelings of abandonment. The warfare was so intense that I had believed God had abandoned me, despite me knowing He hadn't. That was a lie the enemy used. My childhood abandonment experiences caused the enemy to use that. It had me spiraling. When you reach places in glory and your soul has areas of brokenness in certain areas, it creates a mess because glory exposes those things. Light exposes darkness. It was just the perfect storm. I learned a lot. I discovered new things about who God is and His ways. I experienced the reality that He leads us into storms and lands with giants. He does it. He leads us right into these places. Why does he do that? The same reason Jesus sent the disciples into a storm in Matthew 14:22; to

117

discover His glory and be changed. In the story He tells them to go somewhere: the other side of the sea.

The storm comes, and Jesus shows up in such a way that they don't even recognize Him, He is revealing himself in a new way and they think it is a ghost! When Jesus tells them that it is Him and to not be afraid, there is something that is awakened in Peter and he asks for Jesus to call him out, and so Jesus does call him out. Even though Peter encountered fear, Jesus reached out His hand to save him, and asks Him why he doubted? It says that all who were in the boat came into a deeper revelation that Jesus was the Son of God. This is also the journey He invites us into. He will call us to go to places where there is a storm so that we can see Him in a way that we have never seen Him. When we see Him, we are awakened more into who we are. 2 Corinthians 3:18 says as we behold Him we become like Him, and we are changed into His image from glory to glory.

Peter saw this fearless one, and it awakened fearlessness in him. As Peter stepped out of the boat and encountered the waves, the fear he had on the inside of him was revealed. Fear is never conquered by one act of faith. Fear is conquered as we continue to step out. When we do, we grow more and more into the revelation of who He is. With every act of faith in a storm, we see His perfect love and know that He can be trusted. This process is so important. This is the place we not only discover more of who He is, but also who we are. The more storms you walk through, the more you discover that you also have authority to calm the waves. We do not discover this by just watching storms and getting a revelation that we have authority. No, we come into the truth of who we are by going through it. Going through is the place we come alive. We were made for this. We were not made to play it safe. We were created to run and conquer with him.

The process is not easy, but once you learn that this is His way, and start to trust Him more, you are no longer fearful of the waves, you become awakened to who you are and that you have authority over the waves. For me in this case it revealed abandonment in me, but I would come to see the one who never, never leaves. I felt abandoned for a moment, but because of going through that I have such a deep knowing of my God who never, never leaves. This journey changed my life, the way I functioned, and how I saw everything, but it took quite a while to recover.

Chapter 10

Overcoming Accusation

As we behold Him we become like Him

Some of my leaders in Kansas City were asking me to come back on staff. The Lord had been saying to me that He was taking me another way. I didn't know what that meant, but I knew it didn't mean I was going to do what I did when I left.

I was going to explore some conversations with some of the leaders as to what it might look like for me to come back. While I was gone a lot of leadership had shifted. I ended up in a conversation with the person running the prophetic department who was the same person who I was going to build the training arm with previously, the one who did not like me. Other leaders told me to speak with him. Little did I know I was about to be dunked in a fire that I couldn't imagine.

At the encouragement of my leaders, I agreed to sit down with him and talk about what they might want me to do. At the very beginning of the conversation, he told me I had a demon. I was stunned. What was he talking about? He knew nothing of the season I had just come out of. He never even asked. My heart was still sensitive from the previous season, so I was devastated. He called in someone else on staff, whom I didn't know well. I came under this ridiculous accusation that in order to rejoin the staff I must go through deliverance ministry and see the leader of the department (whom I had earlier helped develop that same ministry) to get freedom. I went to Him, just submitting to the process, even though I never even wanted to go back on staff! I was trusting my leaders. When speaking to Him about it He just laughed when I told him what they wanted me to do. He laughed and said I didn't have a demon. He said that if that man thought I had a demon, I should go back and let him cast it out of me. This would end up in a meeting with several leaders, my fathers, and this man who didn't know me. I questioned how I could have a demon and for him to show me evidence. He said it was because I was argumentative and would speak up. There weren't a lot of women in the department. Later I would learn that he didn't think women should be in leadership. I sat in this room with my fathers, leaders, who wouldn't stand up for me. Later, secretly, they told me they knew I didn't have a demon, but they needed to support this man because they wanted to honor his position as the one leading the prophetic department.

I felt further abandoned because I had run home to Kansas City on the request of these same leaders to have this ridiculous accusation. The Lord told me to just be quiet and that He would defend me. Meanwhile, the prophetic department was falling apart. There were several complaints from different women that started to come out about the man running the department. He had several things happen, and after about a year he was asked to leave that ministry and had to go back to the country from where he came. The only apology I would get from anyone came years later. I just stayed away and really got much more involved with a different ministry that was in the same vicinity. Even though I was in a lot of pain and felt betrayed by my fathers, I wasn't offended. The grace of God kept me from being offended even though my heart was broken. Through the pain, I somehow knew that this process of rejecting a reputation that I walked away from wasn't over. My "good" reputation was now being destroyed. My role in a community where I once had favor and where I was a beloved daughter was now for no practical reason being destroyed by the accuser. Even though it was so painful, I knew God was with me and that He would use it. I would go to the local prayer room where God would cover me in a hidden place with Him.

During that season I had a profound encounter. What I saw helped me stand and transformed me in a radical way. I went to the Lord and said, "I don't know how to do this." I knew that Jesus was in this, and I needed to keep my heart pure and free from offense. I asked Jesus, "Where are You here? I need to find You here." I had grown in this place of understanding that in order to get through situations, I needed to see where He was. *Grace comes at the revelation of Jesus.* I knew that I needed grace in that situation, so I needed to see Jesus because that's one way we receive grace. I needed to see Jesus in that place. As I was asking Him where He was, I was suddenly taken into an encounter where I was watching Jesus standing in the counsel before He was taken to the cross. I was in the counsel room with Him, and I was watching them yell, scream, accuse, and call him names. As I was watching, I had this understanding that Jesus had nothing but love for them. By revelation, I knew that. I was thinking, "How do you love like that?" I knew in that moment I needed that love and grace He had for those that were mistreating Him. I was then taken into His body. I was inside Him and looking out through His eyes and experiencing His perspective and His thoughts and feelings. This changed me forever. What I found in His perspective was that as a man He was hurt, but there was a greater reality to what He was experiencing.

I learned in that place that circumstances don't define God, and they don't define me. His greater reality was His Father. I was enveloped in this reality of Jesus' relationship with His Father. God can't help but love, and Jesus was so connected with His Father as a man on earth. His Father was His whole reality. Everything was for His Father's passion. He was so rooted in His identity as a Son. He was God, but He was a Son. The love that His Father had for Him superseded every other circumstance. It was His greater reality. What He was experiencing in circumstances couldn't touch Him because He was so rooted in the Father, who is love, so Jesus Himself had nothing but love for those who were mistreating Him. He was gazing at the Father, and He was so enveloped. That love filled Him so much therefore He had nothing left but love. I was a changed person that day; I have never been the same since. By the Holy Spirit I was given in a moment the mind of Christ in a real way. I understood that we had to be rooted in Romans 8:35. Nothing can separate me from the love of God. If we were rooted in that like Jesus was, we would not be moved by other circumstances. My seeing was opened even more clearly to see what Jesus and the Father were doing. My hearing opened even more because I took on the mind of Christ which I knew was rooted in the love of God.

People laugh when I tell them the chemical makeup in my body changed that day. That is how it felt because it impacted me that much. I have never been the same since. My eyes have never been the same, and I see everything differently than I did before this experience. At the time it was painful, but Holy Spirit gave me one of my most precious gifts in going through the pain of that experience. I got to be with Jesus where He was. I got to see Him there before His accusers and see His heart, and because of that grace was released for me to respond like Him. I realized even more that day that we don't have to *try to* be like Jesus. The power to be transformed and to respond like Him comes from seeing Him.

This encounter even changed how I teach people to grow in the prophetic. I start all my prophetic teachings and trainings now with teaching people how to see Him. I am convinced that seeing Jesus is the most important foundation to properly growing in the prophetic.

Chapter 11

One Thing

One thing I have desired of the Lord, that will I seek, that I may dwell in the house of the lord all the days of my life, to behold the beauty of the Lord and to inquire in his temple

As months passed, I spent much of my time resting in the Lord and my root system in Him went deeper and I found myself so much closer to Him. He was my hiding place and my refuge. I had nothing else to cling to but Him.

I had come to a place where I really didn't know what God was going to do with me anymore; everything I knew was gone. It was an empty place, but it was beautiful. Looking back, I can see how this was bringing me into a place of greater freedom from attachment to the world. He was setting me free. That was the invitation all along, surrender and a greater freedom in Him. He was rooting my identity in Him and Him alone in a deeper way. My identity never was wrapped up in what I did, but the warfare from Africa, the hospital, and the Kansas City accusation pushed me into the heart of Jesus and set me free from caring about my reputation and other worldly attachments in a greater way.

I didn't care at all anymore about what I was called to. I was free from it. I came to a decision that I was going to spend the rest of my life in the local prayer room and that Jesus was worthy of that. If my life looked like sitting in a room and worshiping Him every day, He was worthy of that, and it was enough for me.

I made that confession to Him, and I meant it with every fiber of my being. I was satisfied with that, and it was my joy. I didn't need anything or want anything else. I wanted to love Him. He was bringing me more into a place of seeing how He defined things. I couldn't define how I loved Him; only He could, and I didn't have to do anything to love Him. I lived in that prayer room, and it was my joy. I had surrendered my thoughts about the future, and wondering what He would do, or what I should be doing. There was no vision for the future, no strategy. I was emptied of all of it. All I had left was a burning desire to love Him and give Him my gaze. I would come to realize that was exactly where He wanted me to be. Emptied of me. It put everything in its proper place. Him first. He is the One Thing. I came to understand a bit of David's heart in Psalm 27:4

> One thing I have desired of the Lord,
> That will I seek:
> That I may dwell in the house of the Lord
> All the days of my life,
> To behold the beauty of the Lord,
> And to inquire in His temple. (Psalm 27:4 NKJV)

Now reading that scripture I can feel all the love in David's heart for the Lord. David had seen Him, and because He saw Him, His primary desire was to continue to gaze on Him and His beauty. I believe that God wants this to be our foundation. I know how offensive this is to many people, just as Mary at the feet of Jesus was offensive to those around her. They look at that devotion and they don't see anything productive. They see waste. They see wasted time, wasted money, wasted resources, etc. They think you should be doing something. I just laugh. I talk to people like this every day. They have not yet realized that we are called to build from rest and from love. Hebrews 4:9 says that "There remains therefore a rest for the people of God" That rest He is referring to is a Man called Jesus. I discovered that when He becomes our one and only aim and goal, that is when we run into His true desires and plans. This all comes from a place of being emptied and at rest. In this place we stop trying and we stop striving. Whenever you come to an end and you surrender, it is just a matter of time before there is a new beginning. This is what happened with me as Holy Spirit was about to bring me into a new beginning.

I had previous relationships with a few business leaders who supported me financially as a missionary who asked to meet me and share with them what I was seeing in the place of prayer. Coming back to Kansas City they approached me again to continue doing that. I was so grateful as it gave me someone to serve. After a few months one of those men introduced me to someone else, and I started working with more people. This also helped provide for me financially.

As I was faithfully working with a few leaders, praying for them and meeting with them, the Lord put on my heart that they needed more prayer covering. They were doing a lot and involved in a lot and I just felt like they needed more prayer covering. I asked the Lord that if this was something that He wanted me to do to bring me another partner financially so I could pay a few more people to pray. There was a poverty mindset in Kansas City with people struggling to buy food. I never felt like this was God. I had this in my heart to see provision. Their time was valuable, and I wanted to see these people compensated. Within twenty-four hours with no effort on my part, He not only brought me one person, but He brought me two people to pray for these leaders. I knew God was leading me into something, but He was not telling me what it was.

FINANCES AND PROVISION

As I was doing this and knowing the Lord was leading me into this, I had an uneasiness related to the finances. When it came to the prophetic, I had that uneasiness. Due to the culture I had been in for years, I learned that you don't take money for the prophetic.

The Lord was starving me into a place He wanted me to be, meaning I was barely making it financially. I was living in a house with some girls and barely able to get by. The Lord was pushing me into this even though I had some offense surrounding it. He confronted me one day. He said, "Michelle, if you, with the prophetic gifts I have given you, had gotten a degree in psychiatry, like your mother, and you used your gifts to help people with that degree and you had paid clients, would you be willing to receive money?" I said yes. At that time, I got so much revelation from God's heart from the religious mindset about how the Holy Spirit works and how we box in the prophetic, while the Holy Spirit is the spirit of prophecy. Everyone should be functioning in the Holy Spirit, whether a doctor, teacher or nurse. No matter your occupation you should be functioning with the voice of God. He was showing me that what I was doing was by the Holy Spirit, and I was helping people. He was saying, "Your gift is your provision." No matter what realm of influence you're in, wherever God has gifted you, that's where your provision is lined up. So many people have an orphan mentality, or a poverty mentality, when God says, *go do what I made you to do, and that's where your supply line is.*

At that moment I knew I was free to be me, and that God was going to supply for me in that way. I had always struggled that there were two sides. The way that I was wired made it to where I didn't have a lot of other giftings or talents. I didn't even know how to type, thanks to being in and out of schools and mental institutions. My gifting was really the prophetic, but I didn't know how I was going to live.

I was taught that we should not use the name 'prophet.' Several years later, the Lord would have to undo that in my life in a pretty radical way. God was saying to me, "You're free to be you, and I'm going to supply for you in that way." The struggle is that people do things *for* money, but we should never live to *make* money. That is a wrong mindset. Jesus really hits this in Matthew 6:18-34. He talks about our perspective. *What am I going to eat? What am I doing to drink?* Those are orphan, poverty ways of thinking. It was saying to seek His Kingdom, and all of this would be added to me.

I would soon learn that everything I had gone through in the last several years not only grew me in a deep love for the man Jesus, but the warfare, including health issues, accusations, and more, was setting me up to step out into a new realm in ministry. He had grown me in love and had set me free from so many carnal desires, even caring about my reputation. He had been rewiring my mind. I was learning to lean into Him in a deeper way when accused and not be offended, by the grace of God. He was preparing me for something.

Chapter 12

Losing my reputation

Losing my reputation would bring a new beginning and a rising forth into who I am.

I had just made a commitment to Jesus that I was going to spend the rest of my life in the prayer room. With that, along with the fact that I had no desire for ministry, the Lord started to speak to me about getting a 501c3 and starting a ministry.

This process started by Him bringing me into a vision that I had forgotten I had six years earlier. In the vision I found myself at the edge of a forest; this was the same forest that I had entered into years earlier. In the vision, I stopped to look behind me, and I could see myself on the journey through the forest. I saw myself at different times with bloody feet and being tired, times where I had stopped and sat under a tree crying, and in many other scenes. In all of them, Jesus was right there with me. It moved my heart so much to see Him there. In my mind, I knew He was there, but seeing it this way brought so much gratitude and appreciation for Jesus's leadership in my life. I saw His kindness and compassion. After looking back, I turned around and looked in front of me. I looked up, and I could see a ray of sunshine coming through the trees. The ray touched my body, and new life came rushing into me. Immediately, I began to run out of the forest where it had been cloudy, rainy, and gloomy. I was running into the sunshine. When I came out of the forest, it was so beautiful. I ran into a field of flowers and found myself dancing and twirling with the flowers in the sunshine. It was exhilarating. It was new life. As I stopped dancing, I could feel the presence of the Father next to me. He told me to look up, and I looked up and saw a large field. It was so large I could not see the end of it. He said to me, "This field is yours." Then he asked me, "What do you want to build?" With an overflowing heart, I replied, "I don't care. I just want to build with You." I then came out of the encounter.

I began the process of getting the 501c3. Right at that time I was approached by another local ministry. They asked if I was interested in bringing what I was doing into their ministry, which was for marketplace leaders. I would provide a prophetic prayer component that would coincide with that they were doing. My heart was so happy about that because I loved team ministry and had no desire to lead. I had done ministry with them in the past and really loved them. Honestly, I didn't pray too much about it, but it seemed like a good fit.

I partnered with them, and we came up with a structure. It was going well. Three months into this the Lord confronted me saying that if I wanted to continue this path, I could, but the identity of what He had called me to do would not come to fruition. He said I could continue with this ministry but that He had never called me to join. I was heartbroken. I repented and had to go through a messy process of pulling out from the ministry. I learned a lot about myself in that process. The Holy Spirit revealed to me that I was afraid of being out there on my own. I wanted to be covered in a ministry because I didn't want to go through the warfare again being out on my own. The Lord was encouraging me that He knows what He's doing, but it was not easy for me. I went out and found a small office to work out of. Later I learned it was President Harry S. Truman's old office. I was in there maybe a month, and the ministry just took off. There was so much favor on the ministry. We grew exponentially in six months; I had soon outgrown the small office. I had twenty people with me praying for leaders on a part time basis. During this whole process I didn't really know what the Lord was bringing me to. I was just following His voice at every turn; I'd go and do what He'd say to do, down to showing me which office to have. And then He brought me into an encounter that I went in and out of for three days. This encounter brought so much understanding of part of what He was bringing me into.

In this encounter I watched as it began to rain. It was raining all over the planet, and my attention became focused on the raindrops. The raindrops were huge and coming from the throne of God and falling on men and women, believers and unbelievers. The raindrops were the essence of God, His very nature, Him, and His Kingdom. As I was watching the rain fall on these men and women, I heard the parable of the sower from Matthew 13, Mark 4, and Luke 8. I was aware that what the raindrop produced in a person was directly related to how he or she was prepared in his or her heart. Each raindrop was the same in its essence, but the results manifested in different ways depending upon the unique wiring and gifting of the person upon whom it fell. I saw a raindrop fall on a musician, and it released the very song from the throne. As the song went forth, it was releasing the Kingdom itself. I saw a raindrop fall on an artist, and the picture was the appearance of heaven. Even more than that, the Kingdom itself was being released through the picture! I saw raindrops fall on businessmen and women and innovative ideas, and creative genius sprang forth. I kept hearing the word "innovative." The way a person was created and gifted determined what was manifested through the raindrops. I saw that, right now, it is already raining. It is not a heavy rain but a light rain. As I watched this rain, I saw an increase of challenges and hard times coming through the weather, the economy, wars, etc. Progressively, I watched the pressure and challenges on the planet increase. As the challenges increased so the harder it began to rain at the same time. As I watched this take place in the vision, the Lord showed me a businessman. I knew he loved Jesus and had been extremely successful, and I watched as he lost it all. I heard the Lord say, "They can't build it the way they've always built it. They have to build it on their knees."

I had understanding that the things that are coming forth from the Father in this season cannot be built by man's way, man's plans, strength, or energy. The only way the raindrop came forth through people bringing forth the Kingdom was HIS WAY. He also gave me understanding of what His way looked like. It was as if I was being fed with volumes of understanding of this. His plan is so beautiful and so wise! It's not just about bringing the Kingdom forward or what He's birthing *but the actual transformation that happens in a heart through the process.* So, as the rain fell on the good soil, these were the hearts that were prepared and knew how to sustain what the raindrop released that came forth out of the place of partnership with Lord. When the rain fell on others that did not have prepared hearts, the cares of the world choked it. There was waste.

After this, I watched as the rain literally turned everything on the earth inside out and upside down. There was a transformation that happened where the Kingdom was birthed as the earth was groaning for the manifestations of the sons of God to come forth. Specifically, it is related to a time era, the time of the kings coming forth on the earth. Right now, the Lord is preparing the kings, and it's all about the heart. As I watched the inside out, upside down transformation happen, the transfer of wealth happened as well. It was the raindrops that brought the very ideas of God that nobody would have known, and the ideas produced that very wealth. It is already raining lightly now, and there are those already receiving and bringing forth some of this. But there is coming a massive acceleration. I saw small businesses, inventions, new sounds, new art, coming out of the Body in a new way. It is the very Kingdom itself coming forth.

Along with this encounter, the Lord was speaking a lot to me about Samuel and giving me much revelation regarding the ministry of Samuel and the School of the Prophets. He wanted to restore the ministry of Samuel. It was so helpful to me to understand what I was doing. It was the realm of the prophetic that walked with the kings and brought counsel to the kings that He wanted to restore. Jesus gave me the name of the ministry: Ancient Paths. He was restoring the Ancient Paths, and the name of our group was Samuel Company. Some people and I were working and ministering to leaders. Part of the blueprint the Lord was showing me was the prophetic equipping aspect of it, which I always knew would be part of my life.

STARTING TRAINING

God had given us so much favor that it started to spread by word of mouth. We grew significantly, and then I started the prophetic training arm. We started doing weekend seminars and six- and twelve-week internships. We were getting calls from all over the country for people to come to our training sessions. When I started this, it was so organic. The Holy Spirit just built everything. We didn't do advertising or marketing. I knew I was in the right place and that I wasn't supposed to leave Kansas City. About a year into this, I was thriving with a lot of favor and growth. People on staff at the previous ministry I was apart of were going to their leaders and asking if they could do my training to be on prophecy teams instead of their trainings. The ministry was also getting phone calls with this request. This was going on for quite a while, so I once again was called into a meeting with a leader from that ministry.

He was the voice for all the other leaders in this meeting. He asked what I was doing and building. He told me they loved me and that they knew what I was teaching was good and that I was their daughter. They wanted to know why I had built so closely to their location. He said they had a proximity issue because they wanted their students to do their trainings. He wanted me to tell their students they couldn't do my trainings if they approached me. I could feel the Spirit of the fear of the Lord, I knew that I could not be the one telling people that they could not come to my trainings. I honestly did not want to touch the situation at all. I told him how I felt and that they would have to be the ones to tell people they could not come. I could feel that spirit of control, and I would not have anything to do with it even though I knew it would make trouble for me.

The conversation was very cordial, not heated in any way, but he was not happy with me and came to me again and threatened me with consequences. I was heartbroken. I was doing my best to just follow Jesus and His voice. It was such a paradox for me. I longed to be submitted; I loved the posture of submission. It felt safe to me, though not with them anymore. I had never wanted to be doing something on my own. In fact, I wanted just the opposite. I loved my fathers, but they publicly rejected me and were doing it once again. The rage, anger, and control from them was painful, but at the same time I had never been clearer on what Jesus was asking me to do.

I believed in honoring the fathers and mothers. The question for me in that season was, what does honor look like? That was one of the tests for me at that time, once again, to keep my heart from offense and bless and pray for them. They did what they threatened to do. They publicly told people that they had to choose. It created quite a controversy because it left speculation about me, further destroying the reputation that I had already lost. I had never done anything in that community to cause a negative reputation. I was a beloved daughter. Here I was being smeared a second time because I was not cooperating with a fearful and controlling spirit. They couldn't be on staff there and doing anything with me, and several people did leave staff with them and stay with me. There was a real stirring up that happened in the natural and in the spirit. It was difficult in the sense that I really loved my fathers there. Seemed so demonic to me, yet I had an overwhelming sense God was going to really use it.

LOSING MY REPUTATION

When all this controversy started, I would hear alarm bells in the spirit, and I would hear *this is a test.* I knew I needed to keep my heart from offense. By the grace of God, He kept my heart from offense. We, as a team, prayed for them and blessed them. And because of the previous encounter I had with Jesus before the counsel, this situation was much easier for me. What started to happen in the midst of our ministry was amazing. I felt like I got a taste of what the disciples experienced in the midst of persecution and accusation. They saw signs and wonders and miracles. We were seeing people delivered and set free despite bombs being thrown at us. The spirit of accusation was coming against me. Inside, the Holy Spirit was present. We were having mini revivals. We would spend twelve hours a day with the Lord, laughing and crying and worshiping and going through repentance. In the room the Spirit of the Lord was with us, but on the outside, it was the complete opposite. Several things were coming against me. There was speculation, questions and confusion in the community. There were so many conversations from people asking what was happening. I had to really watch my words. The Lord said to bless them and not speak against them and to keep my eyes on Him and that He would bless this. I knew God was doing something in me and the ministry at a foundational level. I was moved to another realm with Him. I found my comfort in Joseph in his journey being thrown into the pit and sold into slavery. I found my comfort in David's journey before Saul. I found my comfort in the Word and the ways of God, and I understood that God was doing something with me. My heart needed to stay clean. I remembered Psalm 23, *in the presence of my enemies, You anoint my head with oil.* I knew my enemies weren't people, but that it was spiritual. It was really the devil.

I wasn't moved, and God anointed my head and the ministry with oil because our hearts, by the grace of God, were kept in Him. We didn't move into offense. I kept quiet just like Jesus did in the time of the cross where it says He was like a lamb led to the slaughter, and He didn't open His mouth. It was an amazing time. It was the great and terrible, darkness and light. It was clashing. It was internal wrestling with team members about what to do and just being in the community. It was hard, yet it did something in me for which I was so grateful. Two times I had come in front of these leaders and I was mistreated. However, they helped prepare me and moved me toward the Lord. I see them now as nothing but gifts. My experiences there brought me into a position of being anointed. Those challenges have been some of my greatest gifts. Shortly after all of this, people were rising up and saying they were being abused there and saying they were being controlled. I knew I wasn't supposed to open my mouth at that time about the things I went through with them. I was not going to partner with the accuser against them. There is a time to speak and a time to be silent. This time the Lord was very clear with me that I was to be silent about the way I was treated. He told me He was the judge and I was not to speak at that time or try to get my own justice. I was to restrain.

A couple of years later, one of the leaders came to me and

said they renounced everything they had said about me and to forget it all. By the grace of God, my heart was kept pure through that situation. I never got offended. It was a miracle in itself. God kept me, and it brought me to this place where in Him I found a place of only righteousness, peace and joy. Despite what was going on in the natural, there was a place in Him where I could abide. There's a rest and a peace, and I'm not moved by circumstances. Circumstances don't define who God is. It moved me to a place where I could find a rest in Him in a deeper way.

I believe that I was able to move into this reality by surrendering to the Grace of God, not only for myself but also for my Father's. Just like we all are imperfect, and on a journey, so are all those who mistreated me. All of us that were in that situation love God and have weaknesses we are growing in. They did not mean to hurt me. As the grace of God came to me, and I released it to them, I began to see them as my greatest gifts. What they did was not right, but to this day, I am so grateful for the people and my time there. Those hard experiences created opportunity to encounter Jesus in ways that I would not have without it. I love how Jesus puts imperfect people together and by his grace he uses our weakness to see him, love him, love each other, and to grow in mercy so that we can become more like him. It was so difficult, but oh the grace of God! Without His grace we can do nothing, but He generously pours it out for us. To this day I have no damaged relationships with anyone there. All is healed, except for the man that was asked to leave the country. I have never seen him again.

The ministry God called me to build continued to thrive and grow. God began to put me before more influential leaders and was teaching me how to minister to them. I could write a book on those experiences alone. He tested my heart so many times. I was tested many times about prophesying from a pure place, not caring about my reputation, position, fear of man, favor, or finances. It was about being able to give a word from God not thinking about myself or how any word I give would affect me. So many of the tests I went through were forming this in me in greater ways. Holy Spirit was not only preparing me but protecting me by taking me through the things I went through. When ministering to anyone, but even more so to leaders who have great influence, you can have no room for man-pleasing, fear of man, greed, self-preservation, etc. All those things could greatly cripple you as a prophetic voice, as well as pollute a prophetic word. All the things that I went through were schooling me and preparing me to walk into greater realms of impact and leadership in the prophetic.

FIRST ENCOUNTER IN UKRAINE

Eventually, God moved me more into speaking into nations, regions, and cities. I had been doing a lot of preaching, ministering, and teaching on the prophetic, and one place I traveled to quite frequently was Ukraine. God did something in me before He brought me into the next level of authority. I had been invited to do ministry and a week-long training there. About three-quarters of the way through the week, I remember that I was exhausted, sitting on the front row while everyone else went back into worship. I was just resting in the Lord and thanking Him and looking at Him. I found myself sinking into the earth in the Spirit. I went into an encounter and was taken into the heart of the land. I was in the earth, seeing generations pass before my eyes. There were different time frames. It was as if the land was sharing its heart with me. It was as if I was sitting with a person in the natural who was sharing their heart and struggles and letting me into their heart to feel their pain. The land was showing me images throughout the generations. I began to weep. My heart was broken feeling the pain of the land and the blood that was shed on the land. The land felt so abused and neglected and ignored and rejected. I was weeping and weeping and weeping. My heart could not be comforted. Those around me didn't know what was going on, but at that point I was on the ground weeping. They covered me up as I wept uncontrollably for about 45 minutes. After some time, I heard the Lord's voice speak to me. He said, "Get up. I want you to prophesy."

I took the microphone, and I started to prophesy to the land just as I would to a person who might be standing with me sharing his or her challenges and broken heart. I prophesied over the land and spoke life to the land and healing and destiny over the land. It was a powerful encounter for me. This was fall. They told me later that spring that they saw flowers come up that they had never seen before. Not only was that encounter powerful, it changed me in the sense that after that, any time I would enter a region the bottoms of my feet would tingle, and I would feel an identification with the land. I could feel the heart of the land. Even that night as I was prophesying, I was hearing Romans 8 with the realization that the land is groaning.

The land is crying out and groaning for the manifestation of the sons and daughters of God because it's been locked up in this same hope: the redemption of all things. The land is groaning to be restored. It opened my perspective about our relationship with the land and God's heart and His purposes with people being put in certain places on the land. God sets people in certain regions at places and times, but it's directly connected. We are not disconnected from the land. You and I living in a certain region is directly connected to what God is doing in the land. We partner together with God in the revelation of who God is. As we behold Him, we are changed into His image from glory to glory. When that happens to us, the land is affected. The land aligns with us in the revelation of who God is. As we come more and more into who we are, the land does as well. And I realized that even when God would send me into different regions and my feet would tingle, God would speak to me about the purposes in a region, redemptive gifts, and the calling and how the people in that region are directly connected to that. As I was prophesying to the land, I was prophesying to the people. As I was prophesying to the people, I was prophesying to the land. People have redemptive gifts and callings but so do cities, states, regions, and nations. We are all coming into this alignment and agreement with who God is that's a crescendo and bringing us into that moment of that wedding: the redemption of all things, Romans 8.

SECOND ENCOUNTER IN UKRAINE

Another formative encounter that changed me and my thinking and the way I did everything also happened in Ukraine. It impacted a huge perspective in the way I teach for seers and people with the gift of discernment. I was supposed to speak in a church, and I was in the back praying. The Lord hadn't given me anything to speak on that day, so I was waiting for what God would have me speak. As the worship team worshipped, I went into a vision. I went into this place where I saw the bride, the church, at the return of Jesus. I still do not have human words to explain what I saw. I saw us, the church, the bride of Jesus, who was love. We didn't have to try to love or think about how to love. Just as God is love and Jesus is the manifestation of love, we were love. We were love on the earth. There was this pure love, yet at the same time it was fire and fearful. It had the fear of the Lord with it. It was not soft or mushy; it was a terrifying love that came with a fear of the Lord. It was who we are in the Lord. Hell was terrified of this love that was powerful, pure, full of fire. The fear of the Lord is birthed out of love; it is a child of love. It was terrifying to behold and to see this bride and nothing could stand against her. It was a powerful force.

I was watching in awe but with a terror in my heart. Jesus then changed the scene and took me to current day. I saw the church and the attacks against the church. He told me that it's an inside job and there's self-hatred in the body and there's a sickness in the bride. I was watching these scenes and understanding what He was saying. I kept hearing Galatians 5:15, where Paul is speaking about the church biting and devouring one another that leads to destruction related to the body. I saw the tactics of the enemy to weaken the bride of Jesus. It was an inside job. I saw how we, as human beings, all have weaknesses. None of us are perfect. The enemy is an exploiter of weaknesses. He loves to point out where we haven't been fully manifested in our true nature and tell us it's who we are.

The enemy has a false identity that he wants us to walk in. God has a true identity for us to walk in. Because of our weaknesses and lack of teaching and lack of understanding of the way the enemy works, when the enemy comes and whispers in a believer's ear and points out the weakness or sin in another part of the body, he's looking for us to agree with him and relate to that other person as he says they are or to point the finger. It is the enemy's strategy; he's looking for agreement over the false identity that he puts on people.

I was watching this, grieved, understanding at the same time the plan Jesus has for us to walk in who we really are. Our true identity is actually agreement with Him. It all comes down to how we view people. Everyone has weaknesses and some people are struggling with sin, but God is asking us to agree with who He says they are and relate to them according to who they are. Paul says we longer regard any man after the flesh. He was calling us to relate to people by the Spirit. The more we could do that, the more we would see people come forward. It wasn't that we ignored sin. He was showing me the perspective that we walked in and how to have the mind of Christ and how we viewed and related to them. When we saw a brother or sister who had areas of weakness struggling in sin, we were to open our mouths and confront them for their sake and the sake of the body, but the way we were to do it was in love and not accusation and to call them forward into who God says they are. I saw that's where we were headed as a body. We didn't ignore sin; we confronted it. We were fighting for each other, for the love of the body of Jesus.

There was this love for truth and this love for Jesus that we were calling each other into, our true identity that Jesus has for us.

The accusations might be facts about how someone is acting, but it is not the truth about who this person is. How we viewed and treated people in those moments meant everything. Agreeing with the accusation of the enemy weakens the whole body. Seeing the truth about who God says they are and calling them forward strengthens the whole body. What I saw at the return of Jesus was a bride who fought for each other. That was the power of the love. We were so full of the love of Jesus that we were able to say, *I see a brother or sister in this. God, what do You say about them? How do I partner with You to bring them forward into what You say about them and not regard them according to the flesh?* This means, *I don't relate to you according to who the enemy says you are. I relate to you according to who God says you are. We need His eyes.* Shortly after this, as I came out of this encounter, I had a powerful time of repentance as I preached to this church.

An example of what this looks like for a prophetic person is this: As I came back to the States, I found myself in a meeting with a well-known apostolic voice. Sitting across from him, I could see by the Spirit some things that he was doing that weren't righteous. He was lying and doing things in his life that were not of God. I heard the word over him: chameleon, false prophet. What the enemy said about him was that he was a chameleon and false prophet. Because of certain weaknesses in his soul, he was acting like this in agreement with the enemy. I asked the Lord, "God, who do You say that he is?" I didn't confront him. I wasn't in that kind of relationship to do that with him. I didn't bring up anything that he was doing. I just partnered with Jesus and what He was saying to this man. I prophesied into situations where I knew he was lying. I just spoke truth into situations where he wouldn't have even known that I knew. I watched in the Spirit as things broke off of him. His heart cracked open, and he came into repentance. I got to walk that out in the encounter that God had shown me.

Jesus is longing for us to move into this kind of love where our hearts are not in agreement with the enemy over sin; we are not to accuse. Sometimes things do need to come out publicly about people. But, trust me, if it is at that point where God is doing that, it's because He had already tried to deal with that person for a long time about it. God is long-suffering and patient with us, and when He does expose things in His children that way, it is out of His kindness. He loves us too much to allow us to keep going in a direction that harms us or His children. God was showing me our hearts and in what spirit we were moving in. It was about James and John asking Jesus if they should call down fire from heaven, and Jesus said they didn't know of what spirit they were.

You can have one person doing one thing out of love with a heart in alignment with the Holy Spirit and another doing the same thing in the wrong spirit out of anger or accusation. The issue is the heart. That's what we have to wrestle with and discern amongst ourselves. I have to discern my own heart before I go to confront someone. With what spirit am I in agreement? When God gives me a prophetic word, a word of correction for the body, I need to consider whether I've wept over that. That's a big indication of whether it's in agreement with God's heart. There's a grieving that the Holy Spirit has over a correcting word. If I've wept with Him over it, there's more of a chance that my heart is in alignment with

Him versus just seeing something and coming out with a word where I wouldn't have God's mind or heart on the subject at all.

Chapter 13

Will You Walk Away?

Young eagles can only fly so high. Yet they are created to fly to the highest of places. So, to strengthen the wings of the eagle that it may fly even higher, the owner of the eagle clips its wings so it can't fly at all. While the eagle's wings grow back, they are tied down and not in use at all.

When the owner of the eagle sees that the wings have matured and become strong - he cuts the tie so the eagle can fly and fly higher than was ever thought possible.

After five years of intentionally building ministry with Jesus in Kansas City, I had come to the place with the ministry of being at the height of favor and fruitfulness once again. I was traveling and ministering all over the world. I was speaking to influencers of cities, regions and nations. We had a little house of prayer with regular prayer meetings. We had trainings and equipping sessions. Everything was as fruitful as it could be. I felt like I labored with so much love for the team that I had at that time. Most of them had been with me for almost the whole time, and I had poured my love and my heart into them. Many times, I was behind the scenes pushing them to minister to and pray for leaders. They had grown in the Lord so much. I had seen so much fruit all around. I began to have this strange feeling at this time. I secretly missed the hard places. It seems so strange to say, but I had found such intimacy with

149

Jesus in the hard places of testing. I was longing for the wilderness; I was longing for the place where I had nothing but Him. I was hungry for the place where I was positioned by circumstances to desperately need Him. Although we are always desperately in need of Him, I was secretly longing for the desert again. I remember the ache and hunger for it, but I would not voice it. I wouldn't even think about it too long, but it was there. He planted it there to prepare me for what was to come. This started about a month before Jesus came to me again in a terrifyingly beautiful way. I still remember where I was sitting in my office and the tree I was looking at.

Jesus said to me, "Will you walk away from it?" I knew what He meant; He was asking me once again to walk away from everything that had been built. This time it was different, though, because walking away from a position, another ministry, status, reputation was one thing, but walking away from something I had labored with the Lord to build was a completely different story. He told me it would be hard, full of severe pruning. I felt exhilaration and trepidation at the same time. I knew what He was inviting me into would be harder than anything else I had walked through. I had this sense like when Jesus said to Peter, "Satan has asked to sift you like wheat, and I have prayed that your faith would not fail." He gave me one last word. He said, "Trust is your worship." I said, "Okay, Lord. What is the first thing you want me to do?" I joke that Jesus handed me pruning shears, and He came with an axe. I had no idea what I was about to step into.

Almost immediately after that conversation, I had taken the first step, and then I suddenly became sick with walking pneumonia. It went on for quite a while. I was on a lot of medication, some of which gave me bad responses. It sent me spiraling down very quickly. I don't remember a lot of what happened at the beginning of the spiraling downward, except the warfare was so intense that I wouldn't leave the house. My worried team would come to my house and pray with me. I had so much demonic oppression at the time, physically and spiritually. I couldn't hold anything together. Some of the more mature of my team could see the warfare and the battle and were so amazing to stand, fight, and pray with me. Some of the less mature could not understand what was going on and were demanding things of me that I couldn't give in that season, and they walked away. It was a very painful time for me, physically and spiritually.

Then to have some of those around me that I had poured so much into turn their backs on me started a spiral of loss. Not only did I lose some of my team, I also lost some of the partnerships we had. The Lord had already spoken to me about shutting down the building. This whole process took about nine months of cutting, along with the intense warfare. I had gotten better, healed and off the medication, but the warfare had not ended. It became this time for me of a greater death, closing everything down, accepting the loss. There were moments that all I could do was laugh because, I thought, *how much worse could it get? How much more can you prune, Jesus?* I knew He said it would be hard but how much more? I was pruned down to a stump that was maybe two percent left of my life and everything that I had and everything I had built with Him. It was all gone.

The Lord had spoken to me about coming home to Orlando. After a year of shutting down everything in Kansas City, I packed up what was left of my life. I returned to Orlando and entered a season of mourning. I didn't leave my house. I continued to work with a small group of leaders from my home. I had three people left on my team who worked with me from another state. I mourned for about six months. Everything had died. I was always used to being a person who was created to build with Jesus. If I wasn't building something or creating with Him, I wasn't alive. At this point in my life, everything was so dead. I had no vision and nothing to build and no desire to build. There was a death in me I had never experienced before. I had a grieving and a mourning. Not only was there the death of all that was built and the lost relationships, but my life was completely different.

I had no vision for my future and had no idea what Jesus was going to do; He was not telling me. The only thing I had was what He had spoken to me – trust was my worship. Through that whole time, all I could say was, "I trust You, Jesus."

After six months of being home and not leaving my house and being in a season of mourning, I got the best news. My daughter called me and told me she felt like she was supposed to go to Bethel Church in Redding to do BSSM, the ministry school out there. My heart was so happy. For about three years, I had seen her being in Redding, and I knew God was calling her there. When I got the call from her that she felt like she was supposed to go, I was elated that God had answered my prayers and that He was bringing her forward into who she was in a greater way. She wanted to come to Orlando with me for the summer before she went to Redding to start school in the fall. After a month of her being home with me, we were at one of the local theme parks in Orlando. We loved the theme parks.

Rollercoasters were one of my love languages because I loved to play. It filled my joy cup. This was one of the fun things we always did together. We were going almost every weekend. One of these weekends my nephew had come to town, so we decided to go. We were on what I thought was one of the milder rides, not a rollercoaster. I found out later about its dangers. On this simulator ride, I started to choke and couldn't breathe. I was screaming to get off the ride, but I was sandwiched in between my nephew and my daughter in a closed-in car where nobody could hear us. They were panicked because they didn't know what was going on with me.

After the ride, I sat down to try to catch my breath and slow my heart rate. Not feeling right, we decided to go to a restaurant to relax. As I tried to eat, I choked on my food. It wouldn't go down. We decided to find a first aid area because I was having a hard time breathing. On the way, I passed out. They called an ambulance, and when I got to the hospital, I found out that I was having mini-seizures. The doctor said it was because of the G force of the ride. they said that they had seen more patients in the emergency room because of that ride than any other. Even though you don't feel like you're spinning, it's intense spinning. It is what they do to prepare people for space. Because of that ride, they said that I had reinjured my brain from my car accident. My brain was swollen. For several months after that, I was in and out of the hospital. They had me on several medications that kept me in bed. It was one of the scariest times of my life because I could not communicate, think, or have a conversation.

My memory was gone. I could do nothing sequential. I couldn't get a pot out of the cabinet, put water in it and put it on the stove. It was like someone took my brain and jumbled it up. After several months, it didn't appear that I was getting better. Thank God that my daughter was with me. She was a great help at that time, but we knew she was getting ready to go to school in Redding. My daughter was also in a vulnerable place at that time. and she needed her mom at that time more than any other time. I was barely able to function, and she was taking care of me. We decided the best thing, since I couldn't live alone, was that I would go with her to Redding, California. Right before all of this happened, I had come to a point where I was starting to think about how I was going to move forward in life. I had several dreams before this happened, a series of dreams actually. I saw myself on a platform speaking about prophecy and healing, which was always perplexing to me because even though I believed in healing and miracles, it was nothing I ever had passion for personally. I had prayed for some people in the past and seen them healed. I had been healed by the Lord. Jesus is a healer. It is part of the knowledge of who God is. I love it, but it was never a driving passion for me like the other aspects of the Knowledge of God.

Then I had a final dream where I was arguing with the Lord about going to Redding, and the topic hadn't even come up about me possibly going. When we got to the point of her going, I was getting a little bit better. I could get out of bed, but I couldn't be left alone. My brain wasn't able to function well, and I was still on medication. When I was praying about it, I said, "God, what do I do? You sent me back home, and here I am." I didn't understand what He was doing in my life. I knew I was in His will because He had spoken to me ahead of time. I knew He was telling me to trust

Him because none of it made any natural sense to me. It seemed like everything was getting worse and going backwards. Yet I stayed in trusting Him. I knew that was what I had to hold on to. I was very scared. I went from trusting Him to thinking my life was over. I found much comfort in the testimony of Job.

I thought *trust me* meant I had come to the end of everything and had done what I came to do. He spoke to me and said, "I want you to go to Redding and your assignment in your weakness is your daughter. I want you to forget about your life. I want you to forget about your calling and what I've called you to do. Your assignment is your daughter and to get healing."

There was another reality going on in my life at that time as well. I had a few friends who were putting out books. These were people that I had walked with for years that I had helped navigate through things and to whom I had imparted revelation. I was seeing the very revelation that I had imparted to them come out through books they had written. Here I was suffering loss, and it seemed like my life was going backwards. I was looking at people that I knew around me whom I walked with and served. What I had spent years sowing into them, they were now writing into books, while my life was being lost. I would also see people that I walked with on stages preaching things I had preached to them in private for years. Several things created a place in my heart where I was tempted with jealousy, anger, or envy asking, *What about me, God?*

It worked a death in me and a surrender and release. I had to partner with God with gratitude and bless them. I had to say, *you know what? This isn't my Word anyway.* It wasn't my revelation or my word; it was the Holy Spirit partnering through me and given to

155

other people for their journey and what He had for them. It had nothing to do with what He called me to do. I had to resist the temptation to ask God why I wasn't given these things while I was seeing other people receive these things who never had those promises. I had poured into them, and I got no credit for any of it. Yet, I knew it was God. The fact that I got no credit for any of that was the Lord working in me to tell me that it was not my Word but His. I would continually encounter that for years through the process of my death. I would see and encounter that over and over again. It was in my face and happening through something I had poured into them. I felt like it was one of those things where God was being very intentional to work in me, and I attest that I had to walk through with Him. These things actually helped bring me to the place where I despised the idea of having a public platform again. It brought me freedom.

REDDING, CA

The Lord calling me to Redding, California tore my heart and gave me so much joy all at the same time. It tore my heart because I loved being home in the city of Orlando. There was no other place I wanted to be. I had so much love for the city; I thought there was no better place to die and mourn than my home, Orlando. For Him to call me to leave, tore my heart. It was like putting Isaac on the altar. And at this point in my life I had put Isaac on the altar time and time again. It was a deep tearing although the assignment to care for my daughter brought me joy unspeakable. I knew in this season of my life, He was doing a deep, continued work of glory and death to myself as spoken through 2 Corinthians 4:17.

Although I had come to a place where everything had died and I was in utter weakness, He then was asking me, with whatever piece of life was left in me, to give to my daughter. It was this beautiful picture of how He gave His life for the sake of others. Jesus wanted me to love her this way so she would see Him that way. I can't explain the joy to have that call and a focused time to walk away from everything, forget my life and give her mine. At the time I thought I really didn't have much to give. He told me that the action of doing what He was asking me to do would impart a revelation of who He is to her that would last through the generations. So, we prepared for that journey. I knew in my heart of hearts I was coming back to Orlando. Yet He told me to leave and completely embrace what He was bringing me into and not hold on to anything in Orlando, which added another level of surrender. I let go of everything and sold everything. He wanted me to be present in Redding. He wanted surrender and my trust. It was my worship. We got there, and there was no greater joy for a mama's heart than what I saw with my daughter. In times of praying for her, the Holy Spirit would put on my heart to pray for the man that He had for her, His chosen husband for her. Immediately, when we got there, she met him. I saw my daughter come forward exponentially. I would just weep and weep with so much gratitude for the Lord.

It was a difficult journey for her walking that out, and she needed her mom. I was able to be there for her in a very tender time. I saw God do so much in her, and He allowed me to be on that journey and walk it out with her, to midwife her. I felt like I gave birth to her all over again. There still has been no greater joy than to have a season of solely serving my daughter and partnering with Jesus in what He had for her life. There is no greater joy that I've ever had. During those times there, I spent much of my time alone with the Lord. I didn't get plugged in too much with the church. I would go to the services and the healing rooms. I got a little bit involved with the business community and made some relationships. It was very difficult because I was still very limited in what I could do because of my head. In His presence I would receive measures of healing progressively over the year and a half that we were in Redding. My relationship with Jesus became so much deeper and sweeter and with the same confession, *I trust You.* At this point, I was coming up on three years of death. I was left with the little two percent of everything, yet I was so satisfied. I had surrendered even more to the process of death working in me. There's a spirit of death that's not of God, and there's a spirit of death that comes with glory that is of God that Peter talks about in 1 and 2 Peter. There was a spirit of glory that had been resting in me that was working a death in me where, at a point, I just surrendered to it in a deep way. I came to this real place, a tangible place in Him, where I said *the Lord is my shepherd, I shall not want.* I found this place in Him where I had no want for anything but Him even more and no desire for anything. I thought I knew that before, but this was so much deeper and so much sweeter. It wasn't said, but it was a place of – I don't want because I only need Him. He had become my everything in a way that was worked in me through that season. I had so many encounters with Him and of His love and was just satisfied in Him.

I had been there before. It was a similar place of when I said to Him in the prayer room, *If I sit in this prayer room and just worship You for the rest of my life, it's enough.* But this was layers and layers deeper. That drilling of oil had gone so much deeper in me. Even though I meant it in the prayer room, this was a level of satisfaction in Him that it brought me to despising anything else. It wasn't just that I was satisfied and didn't need it. I had come to despise the things of the world, any kind of platform, any kind of thing that was outside Him. I didn't want it. But at the same time, I burned, and I longed and would weep and cry that God would use my life for His name. I had such a deep desire and longing for people to love Him. It was about people loving Him and knowing His name and me knowing Him and knowing His name. I knew I wanted to live my life so that Jesus would have His reward in that people would love Him and that was it. But I despised the thought of any kind of ministry. I didn't want it. I found myself content in a place where I just wanted to look at Him, spend time with Him, gaze at Him, tell Him how much I love Him, wash His feet, let Him wash mine, sit at His feet. I had solely become content with that, and it was all I wanted. He was hiding me.

BACK TO ORLANDO

After being in Redding for a year and a half and doing very little other than serving my daughter and spending time with the Lord, I had gotten much better physically with my head. I had received 95 percent healing. Inside, I didn't have vision for the future or any inspiration. I had such depth of love for Jesus and my relationship with Him. That was good, but He was not showing me anything. I had learned over the years to just be present in my season. Again, I had no need of anything. I was starting to get out more. I had started traveling again, which was very challenging for me being on a plane. Due to the altitude and pressure, my brain would swell, and I would have panic attacks. These were not anxiety attacks but panic attacks. Anxiety attacks are emotional and fear-driven where panic attacks are different. For me, it was a physical reaction to the altitude and pressure that caused my brain to swell and my body to have a panic attack, and they would come on suddenly and with no warning. It was debilitating. Several years after that I would have to take medication so my brain wouldn't swell. I forced myself to get out more and travel more. After a year and a half, life started to come back to me more. The Lord started to speak to me about a shift coming. I had suspected and sensed that there was a change coming. I really didn't know what it would look like because He wasn't showing me or telling me.

I'll never forget the day when He said He wanted me to prepare to go back to Orlando and that my time was up. He spoke to me and said, "Those words I gave you when you first encountered Me—*you are a witness and a messenger of the light and you are a witness and messenger of the truth. You will write books.* This is the year where you are going to do that." He was referencing when I received the baptism of the Holy Spirit over 23 years ago. My first reaction was not one of delight. If there was ever a time in my natural mind when I thought I could write, it was not then. Because of my head injury, I sometimes couldn't remember how to spell words. I would sometimes think one word, but another word would come out of my mouth. When He said it to me, I would dread the idea. This was a mountain for me. I was asked to write an article right around that time for World Changer Magazine, and I can't explain how difficult it was. When He mentioned a book, I did not receive it with delight. The fact that He was going to fulfill a word He had given to me so long ago didn't delight me. It was dread. He told me it would be easy, and I laughed. I felt like Sarah when she overheard the promise that she was going to have a son, and she laughed. I laughed at the thought of it. Normally people get excited when a word spoken over them at the time of their baptism is coming to pass. I did not. I told my daughter that I felt like Jesus was calling me back to Orlando. She was doing so well and thriving. It was time for a shift in my life again even though I knew I still wouldn't do very well on my own. I never told my daughter that, but it was something between the Lord and me that I was very nervous.

To be honest, I was scared. There were so many areas where I still needed help. I wasn't capable of doing my life like I had previously. I was scared, but I didn't want my daughter to know that because I wanted her to thrive. I knew God was calling me back, and I was going to follow Him there. Shortly after I told my daughter, she announced to me that she felt called to go back to Orlando as well, which was another great delight for my mama's heart to come back home with my daughter. We were very close. She also announced that she was getting married, and her future husband felt called to Orlando as well. It was such a joy to my heart to hear that. my daughter and I made our way back to Orlando while her fiance,

Joel, went back home to England for a season until they would get married a year later. Life was good.

Chapter 14

Next

In Him I live and move and have my being. Coming into all that He spoke to me from the beginning.

When the Holy Spirit told me in May 2018 that this would be the year that I would begin to write the books He would call me to write, I considered what that might look like. That began the journey of asking the Lord, "What book do I start with?" Over the years, He had spoken several things to me about different books. I never thought the first book would be about the journey that He's had me on. I knew that one day I would write that book, but I never thought it would be the first book. It was a little unnerving in a sense, even the title. He gave me the title of the book: *Psychic to Prophet.* I didn't like the title because I knew it was controversial on so many levels in the New Age realm and in the church. I had even struggled with the word 'prophet' even though years prior God had really dealt with me about who He says I am. It was really taught to me and ingrained in me that we don't take titles. Don't be named an apostle or prophet. It was alright if you were a pastor, teacher or evangelist but not an apostle or prophet. I took that and received that myself. That was the culture around me as I grew through the years. I received it, took it, and believed it. I thought, *we are friends of God; we are the bride of Jesus, and we don't need these titles of 'apostle'*

163

and 'prophet.' I didn't really care, to be honest. I didn't think much about it.

Then God brought me into dealings where I would be in circles where people would call me a prophet or prophetess, and I'd be offended by it. I'd be thinking, *Ouch, don't say that.* They were trying to honor me. God really started to deal with me about my heart. He said, "This is what I say about you." He had shown me that if I didn't receive this part of my identity and take it and allow it to be spoken over me, I would never fully walk in it. It was so offensive to me. I didn't realize how much I had a religious spirit in me related to those things. There's a movement out there that really puts an emphasis on titles; then there's the movement that goes the other extreme of the nameless and faceless with no titles. God told me both were wrong; both were not right. He said there are those who think they have to honor the title, and they have no idea about their identity in Christ. They don't know that they're sons and daughters, and they misuse their titles. You also have those over here that are nameless and faceless. God says, *that is not Me.* God says, *I'm not in agreement with that.* He told me that the same spirit working in the world related to identity crisis, related to gender with a girl saying she's a boy and a boy saying he's a girl, that confusion over identity, is the same spirit working in the church. It just has a different face, and it calls us nameless and faceless and says we don't need titles. God said, *no, that is not Me. You are not nameless and faceless. I called you a prophet, and you need to step in that and walk in that.* He showed me the importance of the titles and that He created them and that He has the title of the Father. Fathers, mothers, teachers, sisters have titles; titles are necessary for boundary lines and honor and not only in the natural, but in the spirit. I had been blocking receiving more of who I am and what God says about me by refusing that name of prophet to be attached to me. I cannot tell you how offensive and difficult it was for me to receive that.

It revealed that religious spirit working inside me that needed to be worked out of me. I felt like that may have been one of the reasons for writing this book first. God was blasting something over me. I need to be free from what people think or say regarding the title "prophet."

On this journey of these things that I've walked through with God, I have experienced Him bringing things to me and then me letting go and bringing me to position and having me walk away and giving me something and asking me to sacrifice it. I've lived these gains and losses. Paul says, "I've learned to be content in all things." I have need; I don't have need. I've learned to have need of nothing but Jesus. I have no desire for anything but Jesus. Agenda has been killed in me. It's difficult for me even in this season. I would be content to hide in a room, never be known and write so people would know Jesus. He's worked this place in me where I, through this process, have been set free to a degree from the things of the world. He answered that cry that He put in me from that day when I read Matthew 7 and realized, *Jesus, I don't know You. Do whatever You need to do in my life for me to know You like You're asking me to know You, to be in love with You, and to recognize that barrenness in my life.* In my journey, every single thing He did was answering that one prayer: to know Him and to love Him.

He was causing me to know Him and fall in love with Him and freely give every piece of my heart and life to Him without ever expecting or needing anything in return. Does He give it? Absolutely, but I don't need it. That's what He's doing, and that's what He's worked in me. I can say today that I know Him. I know the Man, Jesus. I know the One who's alive. I love Him more than any other person in this world. My greatest desire is to give Him my life. That is what He's worked in me. It's not just words. It's not just a prayer I prayed. I truly know this beautiful Man intimately. Like Paul says: *"I boast in the fact that I know Him"* I don't think this is something that we can do on our own. I know we cannot do this in our own strength. It's a work of the Holy Spirit to lead us on the journey of the way He chooses to form us and fashion us and bring us forward in love.

What I've come to discover is that following Him to this place of surrender and trust over and over again is that I am so grateful for the years of death. When the only thing I had was where Jesus said, *"Trust is your worship."* All I could say was, *Jesus, I trust You.* Jesus did something in my root system. I so completely trust Him. It's done something to my eyes; it's changed the way I see everything. I can truly say I have no want for anything. The Lord is my Shepherd, I shall not want.

REBUILDING

Currently, I find myself in a season where God is rebuilding. I remember immediately after I had lost everything and returned to Florida. I saw Todd Bentley who prayed and prophesied over me with such intensity, nearly screaming over me, saying, "Listen to me. Listen to me." He described an angel standing next to my right side, the same angel I had seen when I crossed the border into Florida. "I'm telling you the glory of the latter house will be greater than the former. Listen to me. The glory of the latter house will be greater than the former." When he said it, I didn't want to hear it. The thought of rebuilding was not something I wanted to hear. I find myself in a season now where God is starting to fulfill things that He had spoken to me at the very beginning of my journey with Him, over twenty years later.

I'm probably the weakest that I have ever been, and He worked that in me. I find my strength in Him. I really understand that Song of Solomon 8: *who is this coming out of the wilderness, leaning on her beloved.* I do a lot of leaning because I've been made very weak. It's so against human nature to think that I've got to be strong and capable and have it all together; then I'm going to walk in the things God has promised me. I find that it's quite the opposite. The more we come into Jesus, the more we discover how not together we are and how beautiful He finds our weakness. That's what He's after. I've never been weaker, yet I've never been stronger in Him, and I have never had more oil. I have never been so in love.

We are rebuilding our school, School of The Seers. I find my greatest delight in my daughter who's now married to a wonderful man. They work with me in the ministry, and they are leading out our prophetic school as we rebuild that. I find myself looking back over my life, and I'm amazed that there's a little girl who goes into her closet and talks to the One she loves. He tells her His secrets. He shows her what He's doing. I get to come out of that place, and I get to speak to people who have influence over nations. I'm amazed at how He does that. I'm amazed that it is love and weakness that He's after. It's not about what we are capable of, it's about what he is capable of. We really come to discover that in times of our greatest weakness.

The journey and process of being in bed with multiple head injuries, sickness and seasons of warfare has worked something so beautiful in me. It's in those times and seasons where I've had to lean. It's by the work of grace and the Holy Spirit. It has nothing to do with my ability, gifting or strength. It's the work of the Holy Spirit. Through my weakness, His greatest power is found. The anointing is in my weakness, not my strength. I laugh now because God is answering what He'd spoken to me years ago. I find myself at my weakest point in the natural but more in love and with a heart full of gratitude for the journey, seeing His wisdom in the journey. I know it's not over for me, but one thing I would say to anyone, especially those who are called to be prophetic voices: there are going to be times of loneliness and feeling cast out, rejected, misunderstood, accused, betrayed, and weak. I would say, look to Jesus. He went before us and walked it out.

Our greatest intimacy is meeting Him in those places. My greatest encounters and the deepest places where I've met Him have been my weakest times in the flesh. Our culture puts so much value on natural beauty, strength, natural capability, and having it all together. Beauty, to Him, looks like a cross. The most beautiful thing we could ever gaze at is a cross that in the natural seemed destructive, disturbing and ugly. It says in Isaiah 53 when we see Him, we have no desire for Him. He's not desirable, yet it's at that place where we find true beauty, true intimacy and true love.

Conclusion

When Jesus invited me to write this book about my journey with Him, I asked Him what His heart was for it and what He wanted to say. His response brought me to tears that didn't stop for a while. He spoke Matthew 16:24-25, "Then Jesus said to His disciples, 'If anyone desires to come after Me, let him deny himself, and take up his cross, and follow Me. For whoever desires to save his life will lose it, but whoever loses his life for My sake will find it.'"

Dear reader, this is the greatest privilege of being born: to freely give our lives. While so many, not knowing who they really are, spend their lives trying to become someone important or do something significant that makes them feel alive, Jesus calls us and waits for us to truly follow Him. Just as the beloved invites the young maiden to follow him in Song of Solomon 2:8, so He is also inviting us.

The voice of my beloved! Behold, He comes leaping upon the mountains, skipping upon the hills. My beloved is like a gazelle or a young stag. Behold, He stands behind our wall; He is looking through the windows, gazing through the lattice. My beloved spoke, and said to me: "Rise up, my love, my fair one, and come away." (Song of Solomon 2:8 NKJV)

He invites us into a fearless adventure with Him where fear in us is conquered, and we become who we truly are: **free**. For me this looks like coming into who I am as a Daughter, a Bride, a Prophet. We are all called to something different. We are all unique. However, the invitation given to us to walk into life and fullness is the same. I, along with Him, invite you to come! Fearlessly come! Forget about your self-preservation, forget about yourself, and yes, forget about what you want! He is generous and will satisfy you with every good thing!

O LORD, You are the portion of my inheritance and my cup; You maintain my lot. The lines have fallen to me in pleasant places; Yes, I have a good inheritance. Psalm 16 :5-6

It is safe to let go and just set your gaze on Him because His mind and gaze is on you! He is an amazing, fearless, safe, trustworthy leader. As you surrender and trust, following His voice even when you are not sure it's Him, you can trust Him, and He will bring you into the fullness of who you are and into all that He made you to do.

Seek to know Him. Love him. Follow him. Trust him.

About the Author

Growing up as a prophetic child with a strong gift of discernment, Michelle experienced the realities of the spiritual realm at an early age. Her journey was one marked with many challenges, questions and discoveries as she grew up to meet the Lord and eventually discover the purpose of the prophetic as well as His intent for her life and gifts.

What she now imparts to others is the fruit of years of journeying with the Lord—of discovering His heart, His nature and His ways, and how to serve the body of Christ through her gifts.

As a Seer, wherever she goes, Michelle imparts clarity and perspective to behold Jesus. People experience breakthrough and advancement in all areas of their lives by discovering what God is like by seeing Him rightly, hearing His voice, and understanding what He is doing.

Since her early twenties Michelle has been an entrepreneur and owned several businesses. After a profound encounter with the Lord, her journey led her to Kansas City in 2005, where she served on the leadership team of the International House of Prayer in the prophetic ministry department. She built, taught, trained and led the prophecy teams on the mission's base. Her time in Kansas City also included seasons of traveling where she ministered in various places all over the world. She also traveled helping other ministries establish prophetic departments, trained leaders and equipped ministry teams to build thriving prophetic communities.

In 2010 she founded her own prophetic ministry that eventually evolved into a house of prayer. Through daily prayer meetings, internships, seminars and conferences, Michelle disciples both seasoned prophetic people as well as those just beginning their journey to grow in their gifts. She also ministers to leaders nationally and internationally.

Michelle's ministry also includes providing executive prophetic coaching to leaders around the globe in various industry sectors— from finance, business owners, pastors, entertainment and media, to ministry and government, including those who have influence over millions of people. She is passionate about people encountering Jesus, as well as understanding what season they are in and giving them the wisdom from God on what to do.

Her ability to impart strategic insight into what God is doing and saying brings perspective and empowerment to people to walk in the fullness of their calling and build the Kingdom confidently in partnership with God. Michelle is also gifted in diagnosing root issues in personal relationships and groups, which include, churches, business groups, and corporations. She brings insight, wisdom, and practical solutions which brings understanding and advancement.

Michelle travels nationally and internationally speaking in churches, houses of prayer, as well as conferences and business groups.

www.michelleseidler.com

Thanks for reading! Please add a short review on Amazon and let me know your thoughts!

Thanks, and God bless!
Michelle Seidler

Made in the USA
Middletown, DE
03 September 2019